LIMITLESS

LIMITLESS

HOW 27 IMPACT-DRIVEN LEADERS BROKE FREE
OF THEIR PASTS AND CLAIMED THEIR POWER
TO SHAPE THE FUTURE

COMPILED BY

ALOK APPADURAI

WORLDCHANGERS
MEDIA

Paperback: 978-1-955811-44-6
E-book: 978-1-955811-45-3
LCCN: 2023907268

First paperback edition: June 2023

Cover artwork: @ d1sk via AdobeStock
Cover design: Bryna Haynes
Layout and typesetting: Bryna Haynes
Editors: Monica Herald, Audra Figgins, Maggie Mills, Paul Baillie-Lane

Published by WorldChangers Media
PO Box 83, Foster, RI 02825
www.WorldChangers.Media

To all the Superbeings who are changing the world by uplifting themselves:
We see you. We hear you. We love you.
Keep going.

TABLE OF

CONTENTS

LIMITLESS GROWTH

LIMITLESS PERSPECTIVE

LIMITLESS LOVE

LIMITLESS EXPANSION

LIMITLESS

INTRODUCTION

"ANDRE'S DEAD, ALOK."

My parents' words landed on me like a ton of bricks.

Growing up in West Philadelphia, it was normal to hear the boom of gunshots shattering the night. Our neighborhood was riddled with crime. Crack vials, hypodermic needles, and empty bottles of malt liquor littered the sidewalks. Gangs of various ethnicities roamed the streets, protecting their turf.

In the middle of all of this were the families who, like mine, called West Philly home. Playing outside with friends could, at any time, involve running for our lives. It wasn't an easy place to grow up. And yet, there was warmth there, too.

Andre and I met in the back alley behind my house where my parents had installed a basketball hoop. The alley, our driveway, was sloped and awkward. Nevertheless, the neighborhood kids would congregate there and invite me to play—mostly so they could get access to my basketball.

Given that I was far from being the next Michael Jordan, I was never the first person picked for their teams. Most of them tolerated me, but many would have been quick to beat my ass given the slightest excuse.

But, for some reason, Andre was kind to me.

He was one of the best basketball players of the lot and could often be seen dribbling a ball up the streets on his way to and from school. School meant a lot to him, and he was quietly proud of his perfect attendance record.

He was also known for his ferocious temper. It wasn't uncommon for him to get into serious fights, and it was rumored that he'd beaten one kid to a bloody pulp. No one messed with Andre.

I have no clue why he liked me, but he took me under his wing—and, by doing so, signaled to all the other kids that to mess with me was to mess with him. He was like a guardian angel. I could take on the world with Andre in my corner.

Andre was a great guy, but he was surrounded by bad stuff. Violence, assault, murder, incarceration, and addiction were daily realities for many of the kids in our neighborhood, and he was no exception.

Looking back, I see exactly where our paths diverged. My parents didn't send me to school in West Philly, but instead to

St. Peter's, a private school in Society Hill. I have no idea how they came up with the money. At that time, they were both professors at the University of Pennsylvania, and while such jobs came with a high level of prestige, the salaries—particularly for early-stage professors—were meager at best. Each day, as Andre and the other neighborhood kids walked to school, I was bussed downtown to learn alongside what many people on my street called "The Haves."

It was my first glimpse of the vast chasm of inequality in our country, and the first time I understood the dynamics of limitation. You see, as I would ride that bus out of dingy West Philly and across the city, my perception would change. Evolve. Expand.

At the private school, we wore fancy uniforms. We had to learn how to write in fancy-ass cursive. We had competitions in poetry dictation. Unless you called a rap battle in an alley a "poetry recital," none of the things at my new school bore any resemblance to life back in my neighborhood.

Kids at my school went on luxury vacations and lived in big houses. They had the best shoes and cars and toys. But, most importantly—and this took me a while to understand— they were *safe*. Protected. They didn't have to worry about getting shot in a drive-by. They didn't have to look over their shoulders constantly. They had adults around them who cared about them, believed in them, and desired to support them as they built their best lives.

Wow. In my child's brain, I couldn't find the language to express what I was feeling and learning. All I knew was that the kids in Society Hill had a *way* different trajectory in their lives than Andre and my other neighborhood friends. One environment nurtured endless options; the other killed them. Sometimes literally.

What was the difference? Well, it was obvious: money.

As for many families in the 1980s, money was a taboo subject in our house. No one ever said, "We will not talk about money"; rather, it was a silent understanding. My grandparents on my mom's side, a God-fearing clan from Upstate New York, modeled Depression-era commitments to humility, hard work, and coupon-cutting. I didn't know a lot about money, but I definitely understood scarcity.

Therefore, it was no surprise that, even as a young child, I could clearly see how the limited flows of wealth in West Philadelphia resulted in crime, violence, addiction, hopelessness, anger, and despair. I began to think that, if I could just crack the money code, I also had a chance of cracking the "limitless life" code.

And then, Andre was killed. Shot to death, another casualty of the neighborhood violence. The story I heard was that he'd tried to rob Sam's corner store up the block; as he shouted at the clerk to empty the till, the clerk pulled out a 45 Magnum and shot him square in the chest.

My mom's opinion was that Sam's was a front for drug running and Andre had somehow gotten himself mixed up in that.

Either way, it didn't matter. My neighborhood angel was dead.

My mom took a casserole over to his grandmother's house, where he'd been living since his parents were too messed up to take care of him. While she was there, Andre's grandma talked about his deep commitment to his education.

"He always said," she told my mom, "that if he could just get to graduation, he would make something of himself."

Now, he would never have the chance.

Too many kids in West Philly, and in neighborhoods across America and the world, do not have a limitless future. Without money and access, they are handcuffed—too often literally. For some, there seems to be no way out of the reality they were born into.

As I grieved for my friend, I promised him that I would do well in school, because school had meant so much to him. I would get out of West Philly. I would create new paths forward for myself—starting with the opportunities that were already right in front of me.

And to do that, I would need to crack the money code.

My desire to be a magnet for resources manifested itself as a desire to be a banker. It was with that intention that I finished my high school education and enrolled in Wesleyan University in Connecticut. Making money was my number one priority. I was entrepreneurial from the start—I created a lucrative business selling pot to my dorm mates—and knew that wealth was in the cards for me.

A trip to India changed all that. I share the full story of that transformational moment in my book, *Maximum Impact Potential*—but the result was that, when I returned to school,

I radically rebuilt my major from the ground up. Cracking the money code for my benefit alone would never bring me the limitless feeling I desired to experience. In order to live a fulfilling, meaningful life, I needed to serve and uplift others. I began to associate a desire for money with a desire for contribution.

As I studied the lives of Mahatma Gandhi, Mother Teresa, and other great philanthropists, I realized that serving others would never get old. It created a feeling in my body that had a limitless, positive, repeatable effect on my mind, heart, and soul. I vowed that I would become someone who could move flows of money in order to create opportunities for others. The threshold for contribution was far less than I had imagined. For ten cents, I could feed someone a meal through Feeding America, a national food-bank organization. For just $50, less than the price of ten Starbucks lattes, I could cure blindness for one human so they could finally see their loved ones' faces.

I wondered what it would be like to do this at scale. And so, I began to embrace the identity of being what I call a Wealth Circulator. I didn't call it that at the time, but I felt the draw of such a mission. It felt like a circular economy of love.

What if every kid like Andre had access to a person or resource who could make a difference for them? What if he hadn't been burdened by those invisible shackles of poverty, despair, and limitation? Because I had no doubt that what led him to Sam's market that day was desperation. Maybe, despite his drive to finish school, he just didn't feel like he had the choice to expand beyond that life.

You don't have to have grown up in West Philly to understand limitation. We all have those shackles slapped onto us at various points. Maybe they're the shackles of financial scarcity. Maybe they're the shackles of expectations by our family, religion, or society. Maybe they're the shackles of insecurity that keep us playing small even when our soul wants to go big. For some, like Andre, the shackles are manifold, and the key isn't anywhere in sight. Shackles like those are passed across generations, lineages, and centuries—until one person finds the courage and commitment to break them.

***

One day, during my senior year of college, I tried to come up with a mission statement. I wrote down all kinds of fancy words and complex ideas, but none of them spoke to me.

Then, my soul spoke, and it said the simplest words: "Do good, and make other people's lives better."

Was that it? Could it really be that simple?

In that moment, I found my North Star. I committed to filtering all of my future decisions through that rubric.

A few years later, I was smoking a joint with my friend on the balcony of my Upper East Side apartment. From there, I could see the rooftop of the elite private school where I'd been teaching fourth grade for a couple of years. My friend worked on Wall Street, but he was fed up with the scene there. We were kicking around some ideas about businesses we could start while we took in the view.

"Why do none of these rooftops have solar panels?" I wondered absentmindedly.

My curiosity piqued, I looked more closely. If we could put solar panels on even half of these roofs, they would power a large percentage of the homes on the Upper East Side.

This was a business that would do good and make people's lives better ... and could provide almost limitless earning power for me. Excitedly, I shared my thoughts with my friend, who immediately saw the possibilities.

And so, our green energy company was born.

I was lit up by the concept of creating a business for social good. I loved business, I loved serving others, and I loved making money. This felt like a path to limitless contribution—a way I could have everything I wanted in a way that also fed my soul.

Well, that green energy business didn't quite pan out in the way I intended. Nor did many of the others I started over the next twenty years. I had great successes, but also massive wipeouts. It was a roller-coaster ride of elation and frustration, hope and heartbreak that finally landed me in a one-room studio in Tucson, Arizona in 2016, at what I now know was one of the lowest points in my life.

I had always believed that, with enough tenacity, grit, and resilience, I would eventually crack the social impact code, the money code, and the "limitless life" code. I'd felt close so many times. But here I was, living in a tiny room with my infant son, Sequoia, with barely enough cash to put food on our table, having lost it all yet again.

I read the books, did the trainings, and listened to the podcasts. I stayed up many nights devouring all the information that might help me solve my problems. Entrepreneurs, I thought, were problem-solvers. Solution-makers. Risk-takers. I was all three, and then some. And I knew my heart was in the right place.

The failure of this latest business venture wasn't what was so crushing. I'd failed before, and I'd always gotten back on my feet. But this time was different. Despite doing everything right, I knew that somehow the decisions I was making were handcuffing me and impacting my ability to do my work in the world.

Out of options, I got on my knees, and asked, "What am I *not doing*?"

And, in that moment, the true secret to creating a limitless life was revealed to me.

Ask for help.

Highly-successful people surround themselves with other highly-successful people, and they ask those people for help.

Yet, here I was, going it alone. Not out of some ego trip or manly stoicism; rather, my reluctance to ask for help came from insecurity. I didn't want anyone to think that, despite twenty years of creating impact-driven businesses, I didn't actually know what I was doing.

I had been tumbling along, duct-taping everything together, hiding my doubts, and hoping that this latest round of catastrophe was just a blip on the radar. My shackles were formed by my inability to admit that I needed help. And they weren't just weighing me down. They were also limiting the future of my child.

I never wanted my son to experience the level of poverty and struggle that I'd witnessed in West Philly. I looked at his beautiful face, asleep in the single bed we shared in my one-room studio, and vowed to him that his daddy would never let him feel lack like that.

I whispered to him, "I don't know what I have to do, but I will do everything in my power to change our lives."

I had decided my way to rock bottom. Therefore, I realized, I could also decide my way into my limitlessness.

And so, I asked for help, and the rest is history.

Today, I am living my dream life. My coaching and leadership company, Uplift Millions, has served over 650 clients, circulates more than a million dollars a year into the hands of other humans through salaries, contracts, and philanthropy, and has built the infrastructure to touch millions of lives. We feed tens of thousands of meals and plant tens of thousands of trees each year. We are funding zero-percent loans to female entrepreneurs, and I donate my time to empower those who may not be able to afford our services. Best of all, I am able to provide a joyful life to my partner, Caitlin, and a limitless future for my son, Sequoia. I pinch myself when I realize that my twenty years of commitment have finally paid off.

I wish I could have shared with Andre what has come out of this journey. His arm around my skinny shoulders all those years ago gave me the safety I needed to be myself in a scary world. We didn't have a lot of time together, but I know that his friendship was pivotal in who I have become.

Andre, please know how grateful I am for how you looked out for me. And I hope that, wherever you are, they have a decent b-ball hoop.

THIS IS YOUR STORY

I created this book to bring together the powerful stories of leaders, changemakers, and entrepreneurs who are finding their own paths to becoming limitless in their lives. Each story was written with the pure intention to serve you, the reader, in your own journey of expansion. Each has the potential to provide a beam of light to illuminate your path to an extraordinary, limitless life.

I encourage you to read each and every story as though it is your own. What aspects of your experience are mirrored here, and what can you learn from these perspectives? Also, I truly believe that at least one of the stories in this book is meant specifically for you. You'll know which one it is because you will feel it expanding your mind and heart as you read. Read this book about you.

That said, there will be ideas and philosophies presented within these pages that you may not agree with or relate to. Don't be afraid to leave these by the side of the road. Not every path is meant for all. However, I encourage you to be open, and to let the magical seeds of transformation be embedded into your heart and mind.

Together, we have the power to begin creating a limitless world, one person at a time. That, my friend, starts with you. If you take nothing else from this book, please sit with this one potent question: "What do I believe is standing between me and my limitless life?"

Too many amazing people capitulate in their lives. The shackles get heavy. The road gets long. And so they quietly settle for a life less extraordinary. That "quiet quitting" is the greatest threat to our collective hope. However, the moment we open to change, miracles abound. The simple act of asking a powerful question jump-starts a magical process of change that may be invisible to the naked eye—but which will, if allowed to continue, produce limitless results.

I celebrate you for your curiosity, and for your courage to live your best life. The world is better off because of your beautiful heart. Thank you for coming on this journey with me and our extraordinary group of authors. I look forward to hearing what these stories spark in you.

In gratitude,

Alok Appadurai
June 4, 2023, Tucson, Arizona

LIMITLESS

HEALING

| 1 |

DEREK COZZENS

THE WOLF OF AUTOMOBILE ALLEY

"WHAT YOU JUST EXPERIENCED? They call that a 'widowmaker,' Mr. Cozzens."

The doctor set his jaw as he looked through my charts. Lying in the hospital bed with my arms crossed and an oxygen tube stuffed up my nose, I set my own jaw to match. Just yesterday I'd summited a peak in Rocky Mountain National Park on my bike. There was *no way* this situation was as bad as he made out.

It was June 2020. The world had just come to a screeching stop, and I was lying in a hospital bed in Loveland, Colorado with an oxygen tube stuffed up my nose. However, unlike so many others around me, I wasn't there because of Covid. I was there because of *me*.

Remember "The Wolf" from Quentin Tarantino's *Pulp Fiction*? The guy who would wade into the messiest, bloodiest situations and get it all "fixed" (and maybe knock a few heads together in the meantime)? That was me. Only, I wasn't cleaning up blood and dead bodies. I was cleaning up businesses for some of the wealthiest and most powerful investors in the world. When things went really wrong—when the CFO stormed out the door, the CEO had a nervous breakdown, or the business needed a major overhaul—I was the one they sent in.

I liked many aspects of the job, but it was highly stressful, and I didn't take care of myself. Too many steak and lobster dinners. Too much wine on the plane ride home. Too many late nights and early mornings away from loved ones, with no time to just … be. My health was crap—but it was a price my mind and ego were willing to pay for the money and recognition I was earning.

In late March of 2020, I was working on a project in New York City. I was hustling like crazy, trying to manage my usual workload as well as build contingency plans against the hellish business realities of a global pandemic. I would wake up at 4 a.m., throw together some scrambled eggs with bacon and salsa, and run out the door while still chewing. *Gotta stay ahead of this Covid thing*, I thought.

Things rapidly got worse. On one call with my contacts at the fund, I described the situation. "Guys, the city's shutting down. The National Guard is blocking the Holland Tunnel and the bridges to New Jersey. We need to set up remote work paths for everyone in the office before it gets any worse."

"You're fine," they assured me, with the peaceful landscapes of the Hamptons and Nantucket visible behind them on their Zoom screens. "We need you on the ground there. You've got this!"

They, of course, had fled the city the minute the word "lockdown" was floated. But I was The Wolf, and so into the fray I went.

Eventually, we did move to remote work, and I headed back to Colorado. Then, at 2 a.m. on a Monday in June, I woke up in agony. Pain radiated from my chest up into my neck. I couldn't roll over, let alone get up. It felt like an elephant was sitting on my chest, and I couldn't breathe.

I thought, *If this is how it ends, I'll know I gave everything I had.*

A few hours later, dripping with sweat, I managed to get to my phone. I called a doctor friend of mine and gasped out the details.

"Dude," he barked, "you're having a heart attack. Go to the fucking hospital!"

I drove myself to the ER. Surrounded by doctors and nurses in makeshift PPE, all fearful of the new virus but still there to save and serve, I steeled myself for the worst.

The tests weren't encouraging. My cholesterol was over 250. My blood was like wax. "How you're living right now?" the doctor said. "It will kill you."

Frustration and anger welled up. I was doing the best I could. I was trying to be *better*—for myself, for my family—and for my dad.

I *had* to hold it all together and get back to work.

Sensing my resistance, the doctor continued. "You're a smart guy. You know exactly why you're here. You know what will happen next. Should I just schedule your next surgery now? Do you want to come back in a year? Or six months?"

Holy shit. This guy could read me like a book.

"I'll leave you to think about it," he said.

And I did.

I was fifty years old, at the top of my game, making more money than ever. I was creating a legacy for my kids, booking adventures around the world. Yet, something was obviously wrong. The path I'd been committed to for nearly thirty years wasn't bringing me the satisfaction and fulfillment I really wanted. So, I kept trying to do *more*, to be *better* and *stronger*—and it had landed me here.

How did this happen?

As so often happens when we ask the right questions, I received an answer.

⁎⁎⁎

I grew up poor. Not just regular poor, but cold, hungry poor. My siblings and I were like feral animals. Supervision was nonexistent or, from my mother, violent. I distinctly remember times when we were so hungry that we ate dog food. My sister, always creative, told us to yap like dogs first so it would feel like a game of pretend. Some years, I didn't have a winter coat, even when the air was cold enough to freeze my hair solid. Thankfully, as I got older, I played a lot of sports; I'd ride my broken bike over to my teammate's houses and their parents would feed me. It was through these friendships and teams that I learned to survive and thrive.

I excelled at every sport I entered. Accolades and self-esteem followed. When I made it to the state and national championships, my father would attend my games and cheer louder than anybody else. It was the best feeling ever. I may have been wearing broken cleats with holes on the side and mismatched shoelaces holding them together, but I still scored goals.

My dad had his first heart attack at fifty; it was a natural consequence of the stress he was under. He eventually recovered, but it left our family in a huge financial hole. My mom couldn't do much, and the family wasn't able to support us either; in fact, my mother's father wrote our family out of his will because, he said, "I don't want collectors coming after me for all your hospital bills."

My dad was creative, often building a business from scratch and making good money for a year or so before his own heart disease would sideline him again. There were a lot of ups and downs through my teenage years, and many more hungry nights. Eventually, though, he found his footing—and this time, he'd hit on a business plan that would solve all our financial problems.

You see, in the 1990s there weren't many apparel and

accessory wholesalers in the Midwest. Smaller retailers were forced to go to New York, Dallas, or Los Angeles to buy merchandise in bulk. So, my dad decided to open a massive "apparel mart" where he could warehouse inventory for these retail businesses. He set his sights on a run-down former car dealership in Oklahoma City's Automobile Alley. The building was a mess, but my dad had a dream. He even had the vision to convert the upper floors into loft-style industrial apartments before that was a thing in Oklahoma City.

By April 1995, the final renovations were complete, the merchandise was arriving, and the clients were getting excited. For the first time, it looked like my dad would come out ahead.

At the time, I'd just graduated college and was working multiple jobs from early morning until night. In between, I was learning about life. My dream was to become a writer—the next Ken Kesey or Jack Kerouac. I wrote stories and hung out at coffee shops and pool halls and drank way too much.

Then, on April 19, just days after my dad's apparel mart opened, a radicalized former US Army soldier named Timothy McVeigh detonated a Ryder truck full of explosives outside the federal building in downtown Oklahoma City ... just over a block away from my dad's business.

My parents rushed downtown and found themselves handing out water to injured people and staunching wounds with expensive garments from dad's racks. Two of my brothers donated their work trucks and spent hours searching for victims at the bomb site. Everyone in town was donating blood.

So many lives were destroyed that day. The bombing itself kill 169 people, but the fallout affected thousands more. Many people we knew personally were killed or injured in the explosion; my girlfriend at the time lost her stepsister. It hit us all hard.

My father, who'd been doing everything he could to create something solid and lasting for our family, was once again blindsided by fate. When the bomb went off, it blew out all the brand-new doors and windows in his building. FBI agents later found an axle on the roof that belonged to the Ryder truck used in the bombing; of course, they immediately cordoned off the area, so my dad couldn't get in to retrieve the merchandise he'd so carefully amassed. Beautiful dresses, watches, leather goods, jewelry ... it was all destroyed as torrential thunderstorms left water pouring in through the damaged areas.

Insurance wouldn't cover a single penny. Apparently, domestic terrorism wasn't a "covered event" in the policy.

My dad, who had just turned sixty-two, had spent his entire life getting to that moment. He'd marched down the football field of life, taking chances and getting knocked down over and over. Finally, he'd made it to the one-yard line and was about to score the winning touchdown—and then, some radicalized asshole went and blew up the town.

It was too much to bear. Just a few weeks later, my dad died of a heart attack.

My mom, reeling from the double loss of her husband and their entire life savings, reached out for help, but family and friends were nowhere to be found. Automobile Alley was now an up-and-coming area—in large part because of my dad's restoration efforts—and many saw their chance to acquire his building for next to nothing. I will never forget the entitled attitude of some of the city's "finest" and how they pushed to gain possession of the property. When my mom was at her wit's end, one of her acquaintances offered to "just take that building off your hands." Not to pay what it was worth or cover the $250,000 my mom still owed to contractors— no, he just assumed the first mortgage as a short sale and wiped the other mortgages away, leaving my mom with the remaining debt. She was forced to agree to avoid going into foreclosure.

I suppose some would call that smart business. My dad's former building is now worth over $12 million and occupies prime real estate in Automobile Alley.

My older sister and brother-in-law stepped up to buy Mom's home—our family home—and moved her into their condo across town. My mom now had her daughter and family close, including two of her grandkids. It was an amazing act of love I will never forget.

As for me? I made a vow that this would *never* happen again. I would do whatever it took to change this reality—for my mom, my siblings, and myself. The day my father died, The Wolf inside me came out, and he was hungry.

That year, I learned what I was *really* capable of. I'd always been a hard worker and had dabbled as an entrepreneur, but now I got scrappy. I quit drinking and focused on becoming the best version of me I could become. I was *not* going to let this cycle of poverty and catastrophe continue.

My dream was to be rich—and if there was one thing I knew how to do, it was hustle. However, hustling doesn't always get you where you want to go. I quickly realized that it would be far easier to get to the top of the food chain as a business leader. So, my dreams of becoming a writer and telling stories quickly went in the trash can. Instead, I joined the corporate world, first in international marketing and then in international finance. While working full-time at a multinational manufacturing firm, I earned an International MBA with a Finance Specialization.

I know now that this was absolutely my path. I was really good at what I did, getting promoted several times while still taking graduate classes at night. I knew what I could count on: my own hard work, intelligence, creativity, and ability to take care of myself and my family. What I couldn't count on was help. From anyone.

I picked up that football my dad had dropped at the one-yard line, and I carried it for him. I made a name for myself inside the corporate ranks. I sat in almost every seat in the accounting and finance departments and rose to be the Global Controller of a couple of large multinational companies. My entrance into private equity wasn't through an Ivy League undergrad degree or my fraternity; rather, it came through proving my leadership and stacking successes one on top of the other. I became valued for what I brought to the table as an operator—and, later, for my ability to lead a team to success and save the day when things were going south. Each successful project opened multiple new doors of opportunity. I was truly at the top of my game.

And yet, here I was, wrapped in a hospital gown, plugged into monitors and drips. Fifty years old—the same age as my dad when he had his first heart attack. Was this *really* all life held for me? Or was there something more out there that I had yet to discover?

I didn't know. But I was going to find out.

When the doctor returned later that day, I asked him, "What do I need to do to *never* come back here?"

He told me. And I listened.

The first thing I did was call the fund and tell them I wasn't able to come back for at least a year while I took care of my health. Within a few weeks, they hired a team of leaders to take over my roles, including a CEO, CFO, and operations team. I coached and guided the new team through critical short-term steps, so they were prepared to succeed in the long run.

Then, while working remotely from my home office in the mountains of Colorado, I set about healing my body from the inside out. I meditated. I spent time in nature. I went fully vegan—no easy feat for a meat-loving Southern boy! That first year, I lost fifty pounds and reclaimed the creative, visionary parts of me I'd thought were lost.

It was an adventure, but it wasn't all fun. Now, I had to contend with the fallout from people who didn't understand my choice to step away from the success I'd created. There was also a lot of internal reframing; I went from thinking

I was doing everything right for myself, my clients, and my family, to understanding that I hadn't been doing right by my soul, the planet, or the people outside of my insular world of profit and loss.

I started clearing away all the clutter and false beliefs I'd put on myself—that I was just a poor kid who had to fight and win, that I couldn't stop to take a breath, that my health was not important, that I didn't deserve wealth and success unless I hustled twice as hard as everyone else. More, I started examining things that had always bothered me about the world of private equity and investments but that I'd never allowed myself to dwell on. Did business *really* have to be all about the bottom line, numbers, and percentages? What if business could be used as a model to regenerate resources rather than just extract them, and to uplift people like my mom and dad instead of take advantage of them? The more I sat with these questions, the more I realized that *I* wanted to be that agent of change, and to spend the rest of my life creating opportunities for people who otherwise wouldn't be given a shot.

Today, I'm no longer The Wolf I once was. Instead, I've become The Lion. I am gathering a pride of leaders, investors, and visionaries who want to work differently and design holistic, regenerative ways of creating products and profits. With knowledge gained from decades in the private equity sector, I am helping to build sustainable, eco-friendly businesses that provide unprecedented opportunities for women, indigenous people, people of color, and veterans. We are operating on a new ROI—Return on Impact—where all funds and companies must function as stewards for the planet. It's a model that benefits all, and leaves no one behind.

I'm also happy to say that my health is great. My cholesterol is in check, and my body and mind are both taken care of. Along the way, I've made peace with the events of my young life, and the old version of me who needed to win at all costs. I have an amazing partner who supports me in all that I do, including my ongoing health journey.

As for the loss of my dad, that still hurts—but I know I no longer need to carry the ball for him. Instead, I've created a different playing field altogether. I like to think he'd be proud.

| 2 |

DANIEL DIAZ
MEETING THE
MOUNTAIN

THE PAIN SEARED THROUGH my body like a lightning bolt of fire and glass.

There I sat, pants around my ankles, unable to stand, stranded on—you guessed it—the toilet. The feelings of fear and loneliness swirled together in a cocktail of despair.

It was 1.30 a.m. My wife and newborn son were asleep, and I was stranded on the toilet, unable to move. My spine had twisted at the base, causing three discs to bulge. The nerve pain was excruciating. I could stand maybe two inches off the toilet seat. Any further movement added a pressure in my back that felt like, if I pushed it, something would explode.

I made the one decision I could: I cleaned up and slowly lay flat on the floor. My game plan was to allow the cold floor tiles to reduce the inflammation in my back enough that I could move to a bed.

It worked. At 5.30 a.m., I was able to pry myself off the floor and, inch by inch, crawl into bed.

That was day one of what would become the most painful, emasculating, embarrassing, sad, anxious, and fearful period of my life. For the next 120 days, I would battle extreme pain that ultimately remanded me to the floor, unable to walk. I was entering the pain cave.

The truth is, I always thought I could handle the sciatic flare-ups and the times my back would "go out" and I'd be laid up for a couple of days. I had a herniated disc in 2007 and did decompression therapy—the process of slowly stretching your spine over a table of rollers to help realign vertebrae—and it helped ... for a while. I started a see-saw pattern: I would tweak my back one week, spend a few weeks healing, be fine for months, and then get taken down by another flare-up while doing something silly like opening the oven.

I thought this was normal. So many people suffered from the same symptoms I did. "Sciatic pain?" they'd say. "Yeah, I've got that shit too! Such is life, brother."

I bought into that mindset. *Such is life. Pain is part of it.*

I didn't want surgery, so I assumed the pain was my only other option. *This is how it's going to be forever, so suffer through, bite your tongue, and get used to it.*

Well, twelve years of that attitude brought me to the

breaking point. My pelvis locked into a place where it didn't belong. My spine went with it and so did three discs—which left me sobbing in pain on the bathroom floor that night, and barely able to move thereafter.

I was so scared. I had terrible nightmares of my wife falling down the steps while holding our baby and me not being able to do anything to help. In the darkness of thought, when the pain had overtaken my body, the outlooks I was producing in my head were grim. To cope, I would cover those emotions with anger, berating myself for being weak and for letting myself get to this point.

"You should be better than this by now, Danny," I'd say to myself. "Where will you be at fifty if this is your capacity now? What will your life be like if you can't run around and play with your son?"

Thankfully, I had been immersed in personal development for almost four years at this point. Despite the dark places the pain took me to at times, I still had a powerful hold on my mindset and spirit. It was certainly being tested by my circumstances, but my mindset saved me. I believed that there were answers for me, and that this wasn't the end.

As I lay on the floor, night after night, day after day, I changed my thinking. I began to wonder, *Why am I here? What am I here to learn? What is this experience here to teach me? What is my body trying to tell me?*

That last question changed everything.

My body was trying to tell me something. It had been hinting for twelve years; now it was screaming. My body didn't hate me; it actually wanted me to win. It was giving me signals about what I could change to help it perform at its peak level. All those "random" flare-ups had been messages—emails directly to my heart's inbox.

Now that I knew what was happening, I could see it clearly. My pain was speaking to me of power. Of will. Of an athlete who had lain dormant for too long. The pain messages were there to remind me that *pain is not who I am.*

My pain spoke clearly:

You are not broken. You are powerful beyond measure. I am warning you of habits and patterns that will destroy you if not changed. I am here to tell you that you are so close to having the pain-free life and physical ability you always dreamed of. There are a few things that need to change. You are inflamed! End the inflammation, whatever it takes. No alcohol. No fried foods. No food that causes inflammation in general. Daily exercise. It is your duty to keep this body clean on the inside. Keep leaning into the possibilities. There is a life free from physical limitations. You can have this life! You're supposed to be here right now, in this pain, because you are going to teach others how to end their suffering too.

This was bigger than me. It was bigger than my pain. It was a lifeline. This period of immobility was the opportunity to change my life I hadn't even known I was waiting for.

In that very moment, I made a decision. I spoke it aloud. "The second I can get to my feet I will do whatever it takes to *never* feel this pain again."

My first step? Get to my friend Josh's house. He does

incredible bodywork, and I knew he could help me. I'd know the next step from there.

On December 16, 2019, it happened: I found my way back to my feet. I cried. I smiled. I cautiously moved around, and I made that all-important phone call.

"Josh, I'm coming over. I need your help."

After five hours on the ground at his house, the pain had dramatically subsided. I felt taller and more aligned.

"How do I keep this?" I asked.

He dictated a strict eccentric training regimen. I did everything he said.

By late January 2020, I was bored with the slow, monotonous routines of an eccentric training plan, but I knew I had to stay on the path. Never feeling this pain again would take a commitment that was bigger than me. So, I called in some help.

I reached out to Dan Holguin—mountain runner, athlete, coach, and all-around badass. I had always been inspired by trail running; it seemed like such a cool thing to do. I told him I would run a mountain with him that summer.

Not that I "wanted to." *That I would.*

His response? "Let's do it."

Immediately, my heart sank! *What the hell did I just commit to?! I don't run, can't run, and have not run a mile since gym class.* But I could feel the blend of excitement and nervousness brewing in my stomach—the magic potion of emotions that told me I was on the right path. I had just committed to something I had never done, never thought I could do, and with someone who was *really* good at it. This was the push I needed to ensure I never missed a workout.

After two months of eccentric training, I decided to test my new lumbar strength with a run. This would be my first run—and also my last for a little while. I took off out the door on a beautiful February day. It was 64 degrees during a time of year when it should have been 11. Needless to say, I was buzzing. Well, I made it about two blocks and had to stop and walk back. I had shin splints, my lower back was pinching, and my feet hurt for three days afterward.

Would I really be ready for this run?

Head down, I kept training. It was March 25, and I'd set the run day for July 25. As I was getting ready for my workout, my wife looked at me and said, "Are you going to start running soon?"

The truth was, I was afraid. Afraid of getting hurt and having to start all over again. Afraid of returning to a place where I couldn't walk, and where I couldn't protect her and our son. Being scared was okay, but I was letting it run me.

Of course, my wife saw right through me; her words were just what I needed to push me out the door and onto the pavement. (Christina, my love, you are my angel, my rock, and the catalyst for so much positive change in my life. I love you.)

That day, I ran for two miles. It took me thirty-three minutes. It was the longest I had ever run in my life.

But that wasn't the best part. I had just run ... and *my back didn't hurt.* It felt like a victory of epic proportions. I was no longer an injured, immobile dad who couldn't help his family. I could run.

Over the next four months, I continued to train and get stronger. Each time I added to my distance, I felt like a super-hero all over again.

Then, on July 23, 2020, I flew to Kalispell, Montana to meet up with Dan and run my first mountain trail—only to find out that the eight-mile trail I'd been training for was actually *twenty-two miles long.*

Say what? The most I'd ever run was twelve miles, and that had taken everything out of me.

Dan looked me in the eye, and said confidently, "You're ready for this. You're Daniel Fucking Diaz, and you can do *anything.*"

I took those words to heart as though they'd come from God himself. "You're right," I said. "I am Daniel Diaz, and I am unstoppable!"

And so, two days later, Dan, myself, and two other friends took off into the mountains of Montana for an experience that would change my life, my business, my marriage, my health, and pretty much everything else in my life, forever.

That run was one of the most difficult feats of my life. There were many times when I thought I had to stop. There were a few times I thought I would die. And yet, I persevered.

Over the course of twenty-two miles, I completely rewired my neurological programing. Limits? I had no limits! Anything and everything was possible—because I had just done the impossible and lived to run another day.

Suddenly, all of my other self-limiting beliefs shattered. There was no longer a limit on how awesome my marriage could become, how much money I could earn, or how many people I could impact. It was all accessible—as long as I was ready to dig in and train for it.

Since that race, I have fully reclaimed my inner athlete. I've run over 2,000 miles—on roads, over mountains, and across deserts. By the time you read this chapter, I will have run over 3,000 miles. Every day, I continue to challenge myself and shatter limit after limit.

I don't train for competitions. I don't train for awards. I train for *life*, because my body and soul are wired for more. Ultra-running has helped me remember who I am more powerfully than any coaching, therapy, or medicine. It helps me get better at life because the act of running—particularly running in nature—mirrors the process we go through when we are looking to advance in life. We have a starting point and a desired destination. The path ahead is often unknown. Unexpected situations can (and do) arise all the time. Things will break down along the way—and when they do, no one is coming to save you. The only way out is through. It's not about how you get to where you are going; it's about who you become along the way.

Today, I'm certain that my body, mind, and soul can carry me across the finish line, no matter what happens. On the trail, in the gym, in my office, and with my family, I am limitless.

More, I know that if I—a regular dude with massive back issues, who had never run a mile in his life—can transform himself into an ultra-athlete inside seven months and completely heal his body, everyone else on the planet can too. And I'm on a mission to prove it.

Your own truth awaits. Your inner athlete is ready to come out to play. And when you're ready to meet your own mountain and claim your limitless life, know that I'm here, believing in you.

I love you.

You can do it.

| 3 |

KARISSA ADKINS

RELENTLESS

I REMEMBER THE doctor's words as clear as day.

"Karissa, if you don't change your lifestyle today, you might not be around for your family in ten years."

At the time, my family and I were stationed in Spangdahlem, Germany, where my then-husband was deployed. On a normal day, you could find me outside smoking cigarette after cigarette with a cup of coffee in hand. Once 3 p.m. rolled around, I would ditch the coffee and go for wine or booze instead. I blamed others for the life I had, made tons of excuses, and had pretty much accepted that my life would be mediocre at best.

My early life was filled with fear, destruction, and many

endless moments of hiding under my bed just hoping to survive the day. Growing up with a severely depressed and bipolar brother was terrible. He would hunt me down with a butcher knife, garden hoe, or some other weapon and force me to do things for him that I didn't want to do. As you can imagine, I spent my fair share of time sitting across from a therapist, talking about our family issues. On the flip side, I also had a lot of highs, mostly as an athlete. Every time I stuck the landing, won the gold, or shone brightly during a dance recital, I felt on top of the world.

Then, at fifteen, I became pregnant with my son, Jaden. I was so worried about what my mom would say—how disappointed she would be. In school, I was bullied horribly for being a teen mom, and at home all I felt was shame. I ended up moving into an apartment with my son's father.

In November 2002, I was called into the principal's office. I was dead tired from working the closing shift at my job the night before. The principal looked me in the eye and said, "Karissa, school hasn't always been easy for you, and now that you're working full-time and raising a baby, I think the best thing for you to do is drop out and get your GED."

So, feeling like an utter failure, I did.

Seven months later, I realized that I was, in fact, a statistic—and I was not okay with that. I went back to school to get my diploma. My senior year was rough, to put it mildly. At home in our small two-bedroom apartment, my son's dad started to show his true colors. Aggression, jealousy, and drugs were part of our daily reality.

By 2003, I was exhausted, scared, and done with it all. I was truly at rock bottom—tired of fighting so hard just to survive, tired of being mentally, physically, and sexually abused by my son's father. One night, I locked myself in the bathroom with a razor blade. I got on my knees and asked God's forgiveness for what I was about to do.

Then, as I pressed that blade into my skin and began to cut, I heard what I thought was Jaden crying in his crib.

If I leave this world, I thought, *my sweet boy will be left in the hands of his father.*

I dropped the blade, grabbed a washcloth, and cleaned myself off. There was no way I was going to let this be our life. I promised myself and my son that I would get us out of this so we could start a new life.

Moments later, when I checked on Jaden, he was sleeping soundly. That's when I knew the sound hadn't come from him. It had been a message from God.

Two weeks later, I got us out.

Over the next several years, I started building myself back up—but only to a point. I'd gotten entrenched in the feeling and mindset that I was a failure. The itty-bitty-shitty-committee in my head was running the show. I struggled to find true happiness and balance. I got married, and my second child, Sara, was born in 2007.

And that's how I ended up in a doctor's office in Germany in 2011, having a conversation that would change my life.

I was tired, overwhelmed, and always running behind. In fact, this doctor's appointment wasn't even for me; it was for

Sara, and we'd arrived late. As Sara played on the floor with her doll, the doctor came into the room and started reading her chart.

"Sara is a little overweight for her age," she began. "You might want to lower her daily food intake a bit."

"Excuse me?" I said. "Are you calling my daughter fat?"

"No, ma'am, but we do want to watch her weight and make sure she stays healthy as she grows."

I took this very personally. I had an entire yelling match in my head with this doctor. Then, I came back to reality just as the doctor was saying, "You are five feet tall and 213 pounds. You are considered obese. And if you don't change your lifestyle today, you might not be around for your family in ten years."

Damn, that hurt. Like a gut punch.

Of course, I wasn't about to show that doctor any kind of emotion; I'd learned early in my childhood that tears got me nowhere. So, I did what every hurt and tired woman does: I shoved those feelings of embarrassment, shame, guilt, and sadness down deep inside me until all I felt was anger.

I shouted at the doctor as I threw toys back into Sara's diaper bag, picked her up under my arm like a football, and stormed out of there. Three floors down, tears started rolling. I made it to the car and then let it all come out—all the cuss words, all the tears, all the feelings. It was ugly.

I looked in the rearview mirror and saw my sweet girl's face looking back at me with an expression that said, "Mom is *crazy!*"

When we got home, I settled Sara in front of the TV with a snack and her sippy cup. Then, I went to the kitchen and filled Mommy's "sippy cup" with wine. I pretty much drank and smoked cigarettes for the rest of the night. My nose was stuffy, my eyes were bloodshot, and I was so tired of feeling sad.

After tucking the kids into bed, I went to my room. As I was falling asleep, I prayed to God to help me be a better mom. I asked Him to take my pain away, and for his support, wisdom, and love.

The next morning, I walked Jaden to the bus stop as usual, and then stopped by my friend Jayne's house for our morning gossip, coffee, and smokes. On a normal day, I would have stayed to engage in the negative gossip while downing at least three cups of coffee and smoking half a pack of cigarettes. But today was different. I felt off. So, I said goodbye to the other ladies and walked the block back to my house.

After getting Sara breakfast, I sat on the couch feeling sorry for myself. And then, I happened to glance over at the picture of my mom on the table. For the first time in my life, I saw her. All 320 pounds. I saw her battle with cancer, diabetes, stress, and lack of energy. I didn't see the entrepreneur, or the strong mom who raised four kids, and who was so wise and giving despite our challenges. Instead, I saw my future self: tired, run-down, and full of disease.

And then, the worst thing of all: I saw my kids having to bury me at forty because I was too lazy to change my life.

So, I got up from the couch, wiped the tears from my face, and gave myself a pep talk. It sounded something like this:

Karissa, you need to take responsibility for your life and your health. You need to take ownership of the decisions that you make. You're going to do whatever it takes to get healthy and stay healthy, because you are worthy and deserving of living a better life, and because your kids need you.

Then, I grabbed a piece of paper and my favorite pen and started to create my "health plan." This first iteration looked very much like a "to-do" list filled with habits I would need to embrace in order to get healthy: exercise, portion control, healthier food, less booze, quit smoking, get more sleep, drink more water, stress less, talk to myself with love instead of hate, walk more, be mindful, meditate, create affirmations, read books, surround myself with people who make being healthy a priority ... the list went on and on. And, by the time I had written down everything I'd need to do to turn my life around, I felt even more overwhelmed and stressed out.

Then, it came to me: *I don't have to do it all right now. I just have to be consistent with a few things.*

I decided I would commit to five workouts per week, and that I would go from eating three plates of food at each meal to one. The rest could come later.

One pound at a time, one meal at a time, one workout at a time, I began to shape my new, epic life.

After I mastered my first two habits of health, I added two more, then two more. Soon, my entire lifestyle had radically changed.

Sometimes, I look back on my life and think, "That was crazy! How the hell did I survive?" How did I go from obese and hopeless to being featured on the covers of health magazines, motivating and inspiring millions of women on international stages, and founding a global health and mindset company where I mentor and coach women through their own massive health transformations? If the doctor had told me twelve years ago that I could be dead, but I could also be *here* … well, being dead would have seemed more plausible.

And yet, here I am, doing the damn thing.

Don't get me wrong, I still have tough moments where I feel like I'm hitting bottom. I cry. I feel discouraged. But then, I hit the internal reset button and remind myself that I'm a badass who can do anything, and that the reason I'm going through this challenge is because there is some new skill, experience, or person waiting for me on the other side. This simple reframing restores my faith and reassures me that I'm exactly where I'm meant to be.

The secret to creating a limitless life is cultivating the ability to turn shitty moments into gold. To follow the cues when life gives them to us. To be willing to change—and then, when we *do* change, to show up consistently and never give up.

Today, I can confidently say that I'm one of the strongest women I know. But my strength doesn't come from lifting weights at the gym; it comes from *knowing* that I'm unstoppable, and then proving that to myself over and over again.

| 4 |

LAUNA MARTIN
SHE'S WORTH IT

THE BLINDING HALO light shone overhead and I felt the familiar sting of needles piercing flesh on my lips. Each sharp vibration of the motorized tool thrust me back to the wee hours of a night twelve years ago. I'd prepared for the possibility that the medical-grade lights and sharp needles could stimulate memories from that night, but nothing could prepare me for the wave of feelings that resurfaced and washed over me with every poke of the needle. Flashes of images moved through my mind like clips from a movie as I relived that time in my past.

On that night twelve years ago, my relationship to myself—and the shape of my mouth—changed forever.

The warm July evening air was perfect for a night of festivities. I wore a soft, cotton, goddess-cut dress in cherry red and was so excited that I hopped fences and skipped up the porch steps to my friends' home. The evening started out wonderfully. I felt beautiful and alive, ready for fine wine, gourmet food, and good company.

It was an intimate gathering: only a few couples and coworkers from the wine bar I managed. My friends, the hosts, were regulars at the bar, some of our best customers. We'd gathered to share a delicious meal and some truly special wine from a private collection. The flavors surpassed our expectations.

My then-partner and I were the last couple to leave. We stood in the upper entry exchanging laughs and pleasantries with the hostess as we waited for our taxi. The lights were dim, and other than the noises echoing from the kitchen as her husband tidied up, it was a still night. We felt deeply satisfied; it was an orgasmic feeling, an indulgence-induced state of bliss that washed us all in a warm wave of sleepiness.

As we said our final goodbyes, our friend instructed her Belgian Tervuren (think German Shepherd) to "give goodnight kisses" to me. The dog, who was nearly my size, growled aggressively, lunged at my face, and bit me in the mouth.

Stunned and thrown off-balance by his weight, I stumbled back a few steps. The three of us watched, frozen in shock, as a copious amount of blood pooled on the hardwood floor. I attempted to catch the stream in my hand while also repeating the word "towel" until her husband appeared, carrying one from the kitchen.

We quickly made a new plan: get to the hospital. At the ER, I was temporarily relieved to be greeted by a doctor with whom I was previously acquainted. He examined me, and when he saw my wound's severity and the flesh missing from my face, he made it clear he didn't feel qualified to perform the repair in a manner that would preserve the integrity of my face as I aged. He insisted I travel over the mountain pass (a more than two-hour drive) to a larger, better-equipped facility with plastic surgeons on call. He prepped me with a pack of wet gauze pads and sent me off with a good luck wish.

My partner did his best to support me. He drove the car over the mountain and tried to remain calm and grounded. He managed his own fear and concern. But because of his emotional limitations and the dysfunction in our relationship, he wasn't able to advocate for me in the way I needed—and, in my vulnerable state, I couldn't advocate for myself.

Hours later, settled in at the second hospital, the dog's owners showed up unannounced. I couldn't believe the medical staff let them in before consulting the patient—me! I didn't want to see them, but because I was unable to talk, I tolerated their presence. They were concerned, as was my partner, and I felt responsible for soothing everyone else's emotions. On the inside, though, I was praying someone would show up and make everyone leave. I didn't need or want an audience gaping at the hole in my face. The trauma of that evening wasn't just about the dog attack or having part of my upper lip torn away. It was emotional trauma, of caretaking others and having no boundaries or real support.

Much later I'd realize I simply hadn't had the tools needed to prevent or navigate the situation.

Finally, an incredible team of surgeons consulted with me and formulated a plan to reapproximate the tissue and restore my lip as much as possible. It wasn't until 5 a.m. that repairs began and, due to my naturally low blood pressure, I endured the procedure unmedicated. I felt every single pierce.

That day, my life changed irrevocably.

Back home, with significant bruising and swelling, I was forced out of work until the wound healed. The sutures in my mouth didn't really match the wine bar vibe. Moreover, they terrified my daughter. She was afraid of the ugly dark threads protruding from my face. And now we were both terrified of dogs.

Weeks passed, I eventually returned to work, and the hosts of that party—people I'd considered friends—took me out to lunch one day, clearly attempting to feel out what I might be expecting and if I planned to get a lawyer. I kept hoping they'd simply "do the right thing" and approach me with a plan to cover my medical bills, lost wages, and permanently altered face—a settlement option—but they never did. Nor did I sue them for the injury or the expenses I experienced as a result of the attack; I didn't have the confidence to take that route. My partner didn't advocate for me either; instead, he assured me he'd cover any future medical expenses required.

Unfortunately, he was becoming an alcoholic, and an angry one at that.

Not too long after the dog bite, the alcohol use, verbal abuse, belittling, and humiliation escalated. Every time my partner was home from work, he drank and was short-tempered. On a frosty New Year's Eve in San Francisco, we escaped for a romantic holiday in the city together before his next business trip. After too many Martinis, he became violent, throwing a glass at me, pinning me down on the floor, and slamming me into the mirrored sliding doors of our hotel room's closet, causing shattered mirror shards to cover the floor.

Like the mirror, whose broken glass surrounded my feet, I was emotionally in pieces.

The next morning, as I leaned painfully over plates of eggs and fruit, I pleaded with him to tell me why he was so angry. I hoped he'd be ready to get help and that we could get through it together. Previously, when he'd blown up after a night of drinking, he'd refuse to discuss his explosions the next morning. This morning was no different.

We drove home in silence.

I knew this needed to end, but I believed more in his potential than I did in myself. I didn't have enough confidence to end it myself.

Thankfully, he did. That night, he drank a bottle of champagne and began to yell at me again. We went to bed separately and the next morning he ended things. He said he knew how much he was hurting me, but he couldn't figure out how to stop. I was mostly devastated but a quiet part of me on the inside was so very grateful.

As much as I knew this was a blessing, my immediate

reality was anything but pleasant. The separation left me with a fair amount of debt. Although I'd gone back to work at the wine bar after my injury healed, he soon insisted that I quit, because people flirting with me at the bar made him jealous. Since then, I'd started to build my own business, but it was still in its infancy.

Single, with a five-year-old and over $20K in debt, I packed up our things and found us a new place to live while he was away for work. My self-employed proof of income wasn't very convincing, so I charmed the pants off the landlord to get the apartment. This is how a lot of things went for a while: conviction and charm. I'd created quite a mess for myself, but I was free—and, somewhere inside, I knew I could fix this mess. It would just take conviction and courage.

Eventually, I started dating again. My nervous system was a wreck, though, and I sabotaged every relationship that felt good or had lasting potential. I also began to get very sick. My health declined rapidly, and we couldn't find the cause: was it Hashimoto's? Lyme disease? I struggled to take my daughter to school and could barely leave my bed. I went from a competitive athlete to a barely functioning human.

With mounting medical bills adding to the previous debt, I finally faced the facts and filed for bankruptcy. It felt like an epic failure, but it was also the first step to stopping my self-punishment. It was a huge act of love for myself and a big letting go of the past.

Several years (and several hundred thousand dollars in medical costs) later, something else was going on. While my body was ailing, my heart was healing. With the weight of the debt lifted, I began to hear and trust my intuition again.

As I allowed my inner wisdom to come through, a series of seemingly ridiculous decisions led me on the most unexpected and wildly beautiful journey. My intuition was speaking loud and clear, and though it didn't always appear to make sense, my Higher Self knew *exactly* what I needed. I just had to have the guts to listen. And I did.

I moved from California to Oregon—somewhere I'd never been, trusting the guidance I was receiving. There, various healing modalities appeared on my path—revealing entirely new ways to reclaim my health—including an introduction to plant medicine. Through the wisdom of Ayahuasca, I found community, physical healing, and nervous system regulation.

Every time I sat in a ceremony, I felt more vitality in my body. I also received guidance on what needed to change, in my beliefs and actions, to continue to move toward health and prosperity. I had to make a lot of hard decisions, taking inventory of every thought, story, belief, and relationship that might be contributing to my illness, and commit to changing anything that was keeping me sick. Every plant medicine experience healed my nervous system, my body, and my heart. The plants showed me where I needed better boundaries (pretty much everywhere!), where I was out of alignment with my values, and who in my life deserved more accountability from me—this looked like dozens and dozens of acknowledgments and apology letters. It was hard but the work was working! Slowly, my body began to recover and, little by little, the plants, and the commitment to making massive changes, showed me it was safe to be me.

A couple of years into my healing journey with plants, Oregon and Ayahuasca brought me a sweetheart! One who had my back, loved my daughter, and provided a safe haven for me to take care of my well-being. His love gave me the space to mend. We co-created a love that wasn't rooted in possession or codependency. Day by day, conversation by conversation, I began to trust that it was safe to speak my truth in a relationship. I advocated for myself. I named my desires. I found my voice. I created boundaries and structure that supported me—and he honored all of it. He honored *me*.

I began to experience my dream life. My communication skills blossomed, and all of my relationships improved! My health continued to show incremental improvements, and as I healed, my finances also elevated. I built a successful business from the ground up, and saw dollar amounts in my bank account I'd never dreamed possible. We traveled extensively, making incredible memories everywhere we went. I felt prosperous in every way. I was a whole new me; a confident woman, ready to claim my many gifts, *and* share them with the world in bigger ways than I had ever imagined. I was overflowing with a desire to be of service to others.

A decade later, as this empowered, wealthy, confident woman, I noticed that just as the surgeons had warned, my lip was changing considerably.

All of our travels meant a lot of photos! But all I saw in every picture was my asymmetrical smile and uneven lip, weighed down by heavy scar tissue. The photos became painful reminders of that chapter in my past. My lip was the first thing I noticed in every photo—and I had to strive to look past it to enjoy the captured memories.

The asymmetry and discoloration stirred a sadness in my heart. A sadness that I had let this happen to myself without taking the steps to guarantee that I could receive medical care for the inevitable changes to come. A sadness for the girl I once was, and everything she went through, simply because she didn't know she was worth more than that.

Looking back, I wanted to hug that girl and tell her she is *so* worth it, and that it really does all work out in the end. But I didn't know back then. Only now can I claim it with such certainty.

In September 2022, I took one last look in the mirror and decided it was time. I booked the appointment for scar revision, and paid cash for the procedure. Why? Because I could. Because I wanted to. Because I was taking care of myself.

I picked out a beautiful blush pink, the natural hue of my youthful lips prior to that tragic night over a decade ago, and settled into the treatment chair, preparing for the process. With each pass of the tattoo needle over my lips, I relived the events of July 2010. This time, I rewrote the story in my mind *and* in my body. I hugged that sweet young woman for the entire two-hour procedure. I let her know it was all going to be okay in the end.

Now, she *knows* she's worth it. All of it.

And so do I.

| 5 |

DEB RUBIN

BREAKING
THE CAGE

AS A THIRTEEN-YEAR-OLD, gymnastics and dance were my life.

I was the only freshman in our school's dance company. I was a soccer player. I'd been doing gymnastics since age four and started competing at age nine. I trained three-plus hours a day, six days a week, and I loved every minute of it.

So, you can imagine how I felt when the orthopedic surgeon informed me that I had severe scoliosis, only four degrees of spinal curvature from needing surgery, and said, "We're going to have to brace you."

Tears poured down my face as I collapsed into my mom's lap. I never thought this would happen to me. We'd been watching my spine carefully since I hit puberty, but I was so active and bendy. I'd gotten checked out at school, and they'd said I was fine.

Yet here we were.

In that moment, it felt like my life was over.

My mom, of course, felt horrible—and responsible, since it was her DNA expressing itself through my bones. Obviously, it wasn't her fault, but scoliosis ran in the family. She had it; she'd had her spine fused in surgery and had been bedridden in a body cast for five months as a teenager. Her back still pained her constantly. Her dad had it; he was quite hunched over and had trouble breathing because the curve of his spine compressed his lungs. My cousins had it. My sisters both had it; my oldest sister had a rod surgically hinged to her spine, and had been in a cast for nine months, and my middle sister wore a brace for four years.

Yes, Mom and I knew exactly what we could expect from my future.

Not being able to turn my head while sitting in a chair, because the brace came all the way up to my chin. Not being able to bend over to slurp my soup. Not being able to learn to drive like a normal teenager, because in the brace I couldn't turn my head to see out the side mirrors or move my foot on and off the brakes. Crying myself to sleep every night for months because I was in so much pain.

It was all waiting for me.

My sisters had been through similar ordeals already, so it all seemed almost normal. Every day they rubbed Vaseline into the gaping, puss-dripping wounds on my sides from where the brace rubbed against my skin, telling me it would be okay.

It was like being in a cage. I wore turtlenecks at school even during the summer to try to cover up the brace, but the humiliation was always present. I felt like everyone was staring at me. All. The. Time. My friends still loved me and were there for me. None of them cared that I had to wear a stupid brace. But in the greater sphere of high school social dynamics, I was a freak, and I knew it.

Do you remember the 80s teen movie *Sixteen Candles?* You know the girl with the back brace at the school dance? That was me, one hundred percent. Same back brace. Same cringing awkwardness. It was awful.

Luckily, I was able to remove the brace for "organized sports," which I precociously interpreted as "anything with movement"—including dance, gymnastics, yoga, and driving lessons. For three hours every afternoon, I was free from the cage. I could stretch and bend and flip and soar through the air. This respite was a huge gift, as it allowed me to still claim an identity outside of "the girl with weird metal neck gear." The movement also helped me manage my stress.

Somewhere along the line, I decided that I was not going to accept my mother's and sisters' fate. I was not going to go down the path of injury and disability. I decided to rewrite my own story and take control of my prognosis. I'm not sure it was entirely conscious at first—but I knew my body so well, and it had always felt like a friend to me. I decided that instead of learning to hate my body, being a victim of my condition, or just accepting the diagnosis, I would lean into it. I would learn what my body wanted and needed so I could work with it instead of against it. Gymnastics, dancing, yoga, fluid movement, and spiral unwinding didn't cause me pain; they helped me get myself *out* of pain from the confines of the brace. They let me feel free and expressive—like I could breathe again. And these practices helped me understand my body's imbalances and get curious about how to use movement to address them. The more I tuned into what my body needed, the more comfortable I became in the brace as well. I looked for the spaciousness within the constrictions. I breathed. I surrendered.

Little by little, my spine straightened. I went from a thirty-four-degree curve to fifteen degrees in the brace and seventeen degrees out of the brace. That wasn't supposed to happen. The brace was only supposed to be a preventative measure, a way to keep my spine from getting worse as I grew. But I actually straightened mine.

I started to look forward to my doctor's visits because the X-rays helped me see the curvature improving each and every time. This gave me hope and a sparkle of motivation. More, seeing inside my own body via the X-rays opened my eyes to an entirely limitless universe beneath my skin—much like scuba diving for the first time reveals a new world beneath the surface of the ocean. This sparked a deep awe, wonder, and fascination with the inner artistry and plasticity of the human body.

I found it so beautiful: the serpentine spirals of my spine and pelvis, the curves of my bones, the tensegrity-like art-work—floating in an imperfect harmony of balance that was uniquely mine.

Through this journey of acceptance, my body and I deep-ened our relationship. I learned to work *with* my body and to stay curious as to what else was possible.

By my senior year of high school, I had not only survived my scoliosis ordeal but also continued my career as a three-sport athlete, becoming MVP and co-captain of the gymnas-tics team and qualifying at the state level for gymnastics and diving. I got recruited to several colleges and finally chose to dive Division 1 at Princeton. I also joined Princeton's dance company and went on to tour the globe as a world-renowned dancer.

Dr. Schafer, the orthopedic surgeon, told me that I was one of the top two success cases in his career. Where surgery had once been considered inevitable, now it wasn't even on the table. He attributed it to all my bendy, twisty gymnastics, and to the spiral movements I was doing as part of my own self-care.

What I didn't realize so much at the time was that, while I was physically straightening my spine through movement, I was actually growing a backbone emotionally. I came to a place where I knew that I was not my diagnosis. As I contin-ued to explore what worked for *me*, in my own crooked body, beyond linear pathways and beyond limits, I learned how to be with what is, instead of what I wished was happening.

I learned to soften deeper into each moment, find comfort within the discomfort, and be with difficult sensations in my body and mind in a loving, observational way. I could be in conversation with my body, rather than at war with it. I came to know myself as a powerful creatrix of my own internal state of being. Through my own actions, intentions, and movements, I could literally change the shape and function of my body.

As an adult, I became ever more curious about the body and its workings— particularly the power of the somatic experience and our innate power for self-healing. I traveled the world studying healing modalities, from ancient to modern, including Western medicine, somatics, mind/body medicine, myofascial work, trauma unwinding, bodywork, yoga, neuroscience … anything that might offer a key to optimal brain and body potential, radiant health, and the full freedom of an empowered body. These have become the foundational pillars of my Dance Therapeutics Movement Mastery technologies and certification programs, through which I have helped people all over the world get out of pain and claim optimal movement and limitless lives.

My mantra is, "Change is *always* possible." Even something fixed, like bone, is malleable. There is no separation between mind and body. When we move beyond linear pathways of moving and thinking, and begin to unwind and embrace the spiral, serpentine pathways of our bodies—from the fascial web, the rounded edges of bone and collagen, the snake of our spine, the wave of our breath, all the way down to the double helix of our DNA—we begin to see that our bodies are magical, fascinating wonderlands of constant motion and inner artistry. Nothing in them exists in a fixed state. We are constantly regenerating at a cellular level, and those cells recreate themselves in response to what we feed them, how we use them, how we move, how we respond, and how we feel about all of it.

And, like a snake shedding its skin, we get to recreate ourselves again and again from that interior landscape, and express that creativity into the world.

This creative expression fuels how we stand in the world. From this interior space of constant growth and intention, I claim my worth as a human being, a limitless creator, a businesswoman, an artist. I get to be all of who I am. No one can put me in a box. I've already escaped that cage, and I will never go back.

At one point, my brace was a reminder that I was sick and limited. Now, it's a reminder that I am limitless. I have broken the cage. I am an integrated, holistic being of interconnected systems and slings which work together to create my reality in every moment. All of the things I was told I'd never do, I've done: I've traveled the world, studied dance with the masters, performed on international stages, and lived a highly active life.

If you want to be limitless, you have to be willing to do the work—to get there and to stay there. Healing and physical freedom isn't a destination you get to once and never have to create again. There is no fixed state, only a winding road.

Along the way, I have embraced the process of falling in love with who I am becoming—particularly as I age. Today, in my forties, I feel no limits. If I can literally create my body and reality every day, right down to my bones, what *else* can I do?

***

The other morning, I was teaching spinal fluidity training in my mentorship program. As I meticulously broke down the details of how to engage our fluid core to support our spine from the front, guiding the group through a deepening sequencing of backbends, I had to demonstrate the deep backbends very slowly, again and again—probably six times in a row.

As I demonstrated how to enter these poses safely and come out of them in a controlled, fluid manner that saves the spine and also looks good onstage, I felt a moment of profound gratitude. Not only was I able to effortlessly and gracefully perform these poses but I was also able to talk and engage with the group as though it was no big deal.

For the scared and devastated thirteen-year-old that I once was—the girl who was told that she would never bend or flip again—my current life is both a transcendent victory for my spirit and a radical act of rebellion. Rebellion against our antiquated system of healthcare that doesn't allow for the plasticity of the human body or the resilience of the human spirit. Rebellion against all the people who tried to put me in a cage. Rebellion against the fear that wanted to keep me small and take my power away. Rebellion against staying quiet and being a "good girl."

Even then, some part of me knew there was a better way.

I am the pattern interrupter. I broke the ancestral lineage that runs through the bones of my family three generations deep. I am the living example of what is possible for the generations to come. I cannot wait to tell my children, and my children's children, that there is another way—a way of trusting our body's wisdom and waking up to the possibility and power that resides within.

LIMITLESS
GROWTH

| 6 |

KAREN WRIGHT

JUST OPEN
THE DOOR

WE WERE IN THE KITCHEN, preparing dinner for our two young sons. I was in the early years of my coaching practice, while Mr. X (my now former husband), the brilliant marketing entrepreneur, had been having some struggles with his business as he tried to take it in a new direction. We had been sharing household expenses since we'd moved in together ten years prior, which worked reasonably well most of the time. As we made the meal we chatted, mostly about the small events of our day. Then …

"I won't be able to put money in the mortgage account this week," he said.

I asked him what he meant.

"I don't have money to put in the mortgage account."

"How is that possible? What's going on?" I started to feel panic rising.

"I haven't landed any clients with the new line of business, and I've exhausted all my backup funds paying the staff and covering the office rent. I don't have any personal money available at the moment."

"What do you mean you've 'exhausted all your backup funds?' You mean contingency funds in the business, right, so you can't take a salary?"

He shifted uncomfortably. "Well, not exactly. I've been covering the business shortfall for a while."

"Meaning?"

"My credit cards are over their limits, and I've withdrawn from my retirement account."

"How much?" I stammered.

Turns out, the answer was, "All of it." He not only had nothing, he was in the hole. We were in the hole. And he never told me any of this was going on.

Rather than be transparent with me about the state of his business, Mr. X had done massive damage to our financial situation without regard for the fact that we had a mortgage and two kids in private school. I was instantly overwhelmed with multiple emotions: terror at the financial crisis in front of me, panic at the immediate need to figure out what had to be done to keep us afloat, and betrayal at the hands of the person I thought I could trust most in the world.

I come from a line of independent, problem-solving, pragmatic women. I've long prided myself on being able to handle just about anything life throws at me. But an instantaneous change in everything I believed about the fundamentals of my marriage and my life? Would I be able to handle this, too?

Yes, this was a crisis. But there's another element to this crisis that made it particularly confounding.

What makes my story ironic is that, professionally, I'm in the business of self-awareness. Of life planning. Of overcoming obstacles. Of goal achievement. Of reading people. Of clear and effective communication. Of devising strategies based on an objective view of reality. I'm a master-level certified professional executive coach. I know how human behavior, motivation, self-reflection, choices, transparency, and accountability work.

But, as my good friend Charlie says, "You can't read the label from inside the jar."

As I look back on what I thought I knew and what I felt as I stood in the kitchen on that pivotal day, I wish I'd known and used some of the things that over time have become daily staples in my client work.

Instead, though, I pretty much "coped" myself into full-scale burnout and depression.

I threw myself into solving the immediate crisis, which meant single-handedly attempting to keep the whole ship afloat.

I told him, "Shut your company down. Stop the bleeding. I'll get a job."

I had a standing offer for an executive-level job with a former boss, and it was time to accept his offer, for the sake of my family. I didn't analyze the situation in depth; I just leapt to what I thought was a short-term solution.

I didn't wonder how long we'd be in this situation. Or consider the impact it might have on our relationship. I only knew that there was a problem to be solved right away, so I solved it. At the time I had no reason to believe this was going to be my "new normal."

Scroll ahead a few years—a few exhausting, frustrating years—and I found myself in a midday message exchange with my husband. He'd had a few business ideas since shutting down his original company, none of which had gone anywhere. I was trying to be patient, supportive, and loyal, and on this particular day the conversation related to a dream project he wanted to pursue. The best possible timeline for this dream project, he informed me, was about two years.

Two. More. Years.

Two more years of me earning the money and handling almost all of the care and feeding and activities and school support with our boys as well as all of the day-to-day requirements of keeping a household running.

Two more years of feeling like the walls were closing in.

Two more years of not getting any kind of real support from my partner.

In that moment something clicked. It was clear to me that I had spent the previous five-plus years telling myself a story that, as time went on, had less and less chance of being true.

I had painted an idealistic picture of me as the long-suffering, ever-patient, loyal, and loving partner to a creative, entrepreneurial genius who was just going through a "rough patch," struggling to find his next big opportunity. And that it was only a matter of time before everything would be fine.

But really, we were in a dysfunctional stalemate where I was increasingly resentful that he wasn't stepping up either financially or in the caregiver role, while he repeatedly conceived of and abandoned new "big ideas." While I really wanted to be the kind of person who could accept him for who and what he was, or wasn't, the truth was that I was in a situation that was clearly unacceptable, not to mention a relationship that was operating on a different set of principles than I'd signed up for. And I was angry, broke, tired, and lonely most of the time.

Confronted with the fact that we were likely to be in status quo for at least two more years, my reaction was quite different than it had been back in the kitchen the day he told me he could no longer help pay the mortgage. I realized that being expected to carry all of the financial responsibility meant something different after five years than it did when it seemed to be a heroic gesture to solve a short-term problem.

I was done. I called my lawyer.

With the end of the marriage, I made a commitment to inflict as little additional change as possible on my kids. To that end, I took on a massive mortgage in order to keep them in their childhood home in the neighborhood with all of their friends, rather than uproot them in the midst of all of the other upheaval.

It was beyond tough paying spousal support, covering all of the household expenses, and carrying that beast of a debt. But it was what I had decided, and remember, I'm strong—so I soldiered on.

Until one day—I still can't recall what prompted it—it dawned on me that maybe there was another way. Maybe moving and downsizing wouldn't be terrible. Maybe the fact that my kids were a few years older than they'd been when all the change happened meant something. Maybe my assumptions about what we all needed could be checked and updated.

And maybe making a change that would make *my* life easier would, in fact, be the best thing for my kids.

So, one evening over dinner, I tentatively broached the subject.

"I was thinking: what if we maybe looked around for a different house? Maybe one closer to school? Maybe one that's a little newer than this one? A bit smaller, so there wouldn't be so many chores and odd jobs and things that need repairing all the time?"

I got Son Number One at "closer to school."

"I'd love to be able to sleep in a bit more in the mornings instead of having such a long walk," he offered.

I got Son Number Two at "newer and less to do."

"I hate old things. I'd love to live somewhere where everything was new and worked all the time."

We talked about what would have to be true for moving to appeal to all of us. A specific maximum distance from school. Space for the boys to have friends over. Minimal driveway shoveling and lawn care required. And, for me, a price point that would relieve some of the mortgage debt I'd taken on.

I have enough mystics and spiritual leaders in my life to know better than to question why things fall into place once you get your intentions and asks lined up. In the case of moving house, once I'd accepted the idea that a move would create more ease, the boys and I had a longer conversation about what the right house would look like, and we began attending open house events in the desired area so we could fine-tune our specifications.

We didn't set a firm timeline, but rather agreed that we'd know it when we found it, and in the meantime, we should get our current house ready so we could act quickly when we found the right thing. To that end, I was doing some work in the front yard one day when my next-door neighbor appeared on her front porch. We started chatting and I told her what we were planning—that we had a sense of what we were looking for, and that we had started the process. She asked for details, and I shared some of the key items on our list.

She went quiet, with an odd look on her face.

"Have I ever introduced you to my brother?"

Turns out, her brother was twenty-four hours away from putting a "For Sale" sign on a house that was in the exact neighborhood where we were looking, at the right price, and sounded like it met most of our other criteria. Despite sounding too good to be true, we arranged to go and visit—me with healthy skepticism and the boys with their own lists of requirements.

Crazily enough, it was perfect. Beyond perfect.

We signed the deal. And all it took was being clear on what we wanted, being willing to ask for it, and then paying attention when it showed up right under our noses.

With the deal done on the perfect house, we had to undertake the process of disassembling the home we had lived in for the better part of twenty years—the home my boys had lived in since they were born; the home that housed a thousand memories, and held all of the stuff attached to those memories. To say I was overwhelmed would have been an understatement. Yet, true to form, I dove in and started the process, dumping and throwing things in boxes and generally creating a tornado of a mess.

One Saturday morning, a few days before the moving truck was to arrive, a neighbor dropped by unannounced. I made an effort to be polite, wondering what she wanted.

"I've come to help you pack. I'm good at kitchens."

I'm sure my jaw dropped. And, of course, my first instinct was to decline politely but firmly. Did I want her to see how disorganized I was? Would she pack things the way I wanted them packed? A hundred objections flew through my mind in that instant.

"You need help. I'm here and I'm offering. Are you going to let me in?"

She was smiling, but firm. So, I stepped aside, and in she came.

Several hours later, my kitchen was impeccably packed. It was the perfect gift, perfectly timed—and I had come *this close* to turning it down.

Old habits die hard. And if we expect ourselves to be perfect, we will just get frustrated and continue the vicious cycle.

Despite what I do for a living, I have to remind myself to not only get clear on my intentions but to recognize *and* accept gifts when they appear, no matter what form they appear in. As a result of my letting go of my need to be "strong," the boys and I downsized our space and volume of stuff, I released a big load of stress-inducing debt, and I learned some valuable lessons about what happens when you open the door and allow support and serendipity into your life.

Work on progress, not perfection. And when someone offers help, try saying yes.

| 7 |

GIGI ABDEL-SAMED

FREEDOM IS AN INSIDE JOB

HOW DID I GET HERE?

All I'd ever wanted since the age of eleven was to become a doctor. I wanted to help people, to be able to lay my hands on them and make the pain go away. Yet here I was, in a rehab facility, sharing a small bedroom and one single bathroom with four other women. I was the one who needed help.

Where had it all gone wrong?

I was miserable, exhausted, tired, and lonely. Though I had it all on paper—medical director of a community hospital emergency room, associate director at a level-1 trauma center ER, a million-dollar dream home, a lake house—I had never felt emptier. I felt like it all owned me. I worked to pay for the things I had, but I wasn't enjoying them anymore.

I could pinpoint the moment it all began unraveling.

I stood in my kitchen sometime after midnight, fully dressed, car keys and a crumpled receipt in one hand, my teeth sunk halfway into a Boston cream donut I didn't remember buying in the other. My heart sank. The last thing I remembered was being in my pajamas, in my bed, ready for sleep, but I couldn't refute what the receipt showed me: I had gotten dressed, driven to the twenty-four-hour Dunkin' Donuts drive-thru, and paid exact change for three donuts. Apparently, I'd eaten the first two donuts in a complete black-out and only came to as I was chowing down on the third.

I'd never even tried a drug in my life, and even the stress of repeatedly working through the night in an ER wasn't going to make me start. But I'd started taking Ambien to help me sleep during the day, and I'd only started because it was dubbed "safe" and "non-addictive."

Over the next few months, though, I gradually began using more and more Ambien. I wondered why I was always short at the end of the month, not realizing I'd been waking up in the middle of the night, blacked out, and taking more so I could sleep. There were mornings when I would wake exhausted, wondering how on earth the laundry had gotten done and why the floors were vacuumed. I hadn't done it, right? I was sleeping!

I began to get prescriptions from my colleagues—"You work night shifts, of course," they said. But when that wasn't enough, I began writing prescriptions for myself. And then Ambien's effect on me lessened. It no longer made me sleepy, just calm, and before long, I couldn't even feel that. But I had to keep taking it because I became nauseous and sweaty if I didn't.

One night, about six months into Ambien's regime over my life, I was working a twelve-hour shift. I had one dose of Ambien tucked safely in the breast pocket of my white coat, and I was counting down the hours to be off duty so I could take it in the car. That way, I wouldn't be shaky driving home. But I didn't make it.

In the final hour of my shift, I began to sweat and feel nauseated. I couldn't speak and my left arm wouldn't work. They thought I was having a stroke.

I'd worked so hard to be successful. I graduated from Cornell with two majors and a minor in three years, getting by on loans and working part-time. I'd gotten into the second oldest residency for emergency medicine and survived 120-hour work weeks and no social life. And now, ten years later, practicing as an attending, it would seem I had it all. People respected me and treated me like I was the smartest person in the room. But I felt hollow. Broken. Like I was a fraud. How could I complain, with everything I'd ever dreamed of surrounding me? I felt trapped.

That night in the ER, unable to speak, unable to use my left arm , I faced the hard truth. Ambien *was* addictive, and I could no longer go even twelve hours without going into withdrawal. I didn't leave the hospital that night; instead, my colleague had to take care of me. Exhausted and feeling betrayed by my body, I endured an MRI, a spinal tap, labs, a urinalysis done by catheter so they could drug test it and be sure it was mine, and the humiliation of being sent to a detox facility against my will even though the drug test was negative. After all, Ambien "isn't addictive" so there was no drug test for it back then.

It was the end ... and it was the beginning.

It certainly wasn't easy street after that stay in the hospital. I stumbled and failed many times on my way back to myself. At first, it was frustrating because no one took my condition seriously. "Just Ambien?" they would say, "You can't be a drug addict." And yet I knew I was. When I finally found a facility that had information on their website about Ambien addiction, I had hope again. I made the difficult decision to voluntarily surrender my medical license and enter what could be a year-long stay in rehab. I knew I was at a turning point, and my life could be on the line—as well as the lives of my patients. And that was one line I would never intentionally cross. The withdrawal had caused me to have a seizure and stop breathing. I couldn't go on like this.

My first week in detox, I went three days without sleep, hallucinating all the while, and then had another seizure. But I'd decided, and I wasn't backing down. I would rather die having a seizure than ever put Ambien in my body again.

In the rehab facility, life was simplified and there wasn't much to do. There were maybe thirty of us in the program at a time, both men and women. There were no computers or cell phones, just a television that barely got cable and was only on during limited (and supervised) hours, and a landline phone in a communal room. But this residential facility was on the beach in California, and it was beautiful. Here, they understood what it was like to be surfacing from an addiction, feeling like one raw nerve with the whole world standing on it. They understood that I felt so much shame at who I'd become that even looking another person in the eye felt like unbearable agony. And so they brought me back to life, one day at a time.

Each resident worked through eight modules at their own pace. Time became irrelevant, and yet always present. I spent time detoxing with physical exercise and sweating out toxins in the sauna. There were exercises to help me get back in my body and tolerate being there. The simple exercise of holding eye contact with another person without attempting to smile or relieve the "tension" was profoundly life-altering for me. I'll never forget my first session of this, which was only one minute long. All the stories in my head shot to the surface: "Why aren't they smiling at me? Is something wrong with my hair?" The same internal drive that made me a high achiever also made me afraid of disappointing anyone, to the detriment of myself. Over those months in rehab, I built up to holding eye contact for forty-five minutes at a time. This exercise, and others, were the perfect training ground for taking back my power from the outside world. Each day put into perspective all the things I had thought were so urgent.

Before rehab, I was the effect of everything: I reacted to emails like a time bomb that had to be responded to immediately. Tense meetings made me lose sleep for days before and after. An unhappy patient or bad outcome would keep me up, playing it over and over in my mind. I was living on the knife's edge of anxiety and burnout where everything was a crisis that needed to be dealt with "stat," or preferably yesterday. But doing those exercises, freeing my body of toxins, I finally understood: it didn't really matter. None of it mattered.

I released the weight of those false pressures and stress. Mountains were just molehills.

And I became limitless. Weightless. Free.

I realized that I had lost sight of who I truly was and what I stood for. I had forgotten what made me become a doctor in the first place. It wasn't the money, house, or car. It was the service, connection, and love. It was my way of serving God and love through medicine.

How far I had come from that powerless person. From a girl who wanted to hide and numb herself to a woman who, in her first year of sobriety, lost her dad unexpectedly, went through foreclosure and bankruptcy, and still stood strong in her freedom. None of that defined me. I knew I would never again use a substance for any false sense of calm and control. Now *I* was truly in control.

I had to wait two years to apply to have my medical license reinstated, doing random drug tests up to six times a month to prove sobriety, and it wasn't even a sure thing. I didn't know if I would ever be allowed to practice medicine again, and that hurt. But I couldn't sit at home doing nothing, so I took a barista job at Starbucks. Perhaps some would think it's embarrassing to become a barista after ten years of being a doctor, but I didn't care. I had learned in rehab to take back my power from any circumstance or event, and working in a coffee shop offered something new to learn, a place to belong. My coworkers were my family. Customers would look at me quizzically when they learned about my story, but I shared openly and vulnerably. I had learned the hard way: secrets kill. Pretending to be more or other than who and what I am led to illness.

I made the decision to get my MBA, in case I wasn't allowed to practice as a physician again, and then I was asked to become a manager at Starbucks. I declined, but in that moment, I realized I was not a survivor. I was a thriver.

Everything I needed was in my heart, my head, and my hands. Each day, with each smile on a customer's face as I handed them their coffee just the way they liked it and asked about their kids and families, my self-esteem grew. I knew my place in the world again: one human being helping others. I could be of service even when I was making coffee.

I finally knew who I was, with or without the white coat. I was a person who made every life better simply by being in it. In any way, big or small, I made a difference. And I would keep doing so. I began the journey back to gratitude, back to that little girl who just wanted to make the pain stop by touching a patient. And I made a vow to never again lose sight of my inner compass, my North Star.

Two years later, my license was reinstated. By the grace of God, that was fifteen years ago and those lessons have never left me. I am free and limitless because I was willing to let go of those old beliefs, those false burdens and pressures.

Today, twenty-seven years after first becoming a physician, I am back in the ER, and I am thriving. I embody the calm in the middle of chaos, the eye of the storm: at peace and fully aware, no matter what. But the best part is that even on fully packed days, it all feels manageable—because I put me first. I feed myself first. I fill my cup with connection and love and service, and then it's easy to turn around and help others. I create from my own being.

True freedom doesn't depend on any external circumstances. We all have the capacity to be anything, to create anything—but we hold ourselves back. What's keeping you from your true potential?

I thought I had it all and I felt trapped.

Then I lost it all and became limitless.

Now I truly have what matters, and am truly free.

| 8 |

TOM LADEGAARD, ESQ.
HOLDING THE DUALITY

"WE'RE LETTING YOU GO."

The firm administrator's words hung in the air for a moment. It felt like the breath had been violently knocked from my lungs. My blood pressure spiked; I could feel my pulse in my ears. Time slowed.

After a few moments of stunned silence, I emitted a single sound.

"Oh," I said.

This was really happening. I was getting fired for the first time in my life. I had worked for this firm for six and a half years, neglecting my wife and kids on nights and weekends, basically giving my life to this organization ... and the founder just delegated my termination to a staff member.

I half-listened as the administrator summarized the termination process, cashing out my PTO, the final paycheck, and the single month of severance pay I would receive. My mind immediately wandered to my wife and two children. I wondered, *What the hell am I going to do?*

We had just sold our condo, which we could not afford, and leased a house near the office. We had over $40,000 in credit card debt, plus my student loans, and we weren't even making ends meet on my $130,000 salary, which I had just lost. I was the sole breadwinner who, apparently, would no longer be winning any bread.

As a husband and father whose identity was attached to being a leader and provider, it was emasculating. How would I take care of my family and manage this suffocating debt if I no longer had a job?

I stepped outside to call my wife. She was at the mall with our five-year-old daughter and three-year-old son, buying them new shoes. We agreed the termination was a blessing in disguise since I was miserable and stressed out at the firm. My morale was in the toilet after several promised bonuses went unpaid, and I'd recently heard that my boss was disparaging me around the office to anyone who would listen, yet he was always civil to my face.

How much longer could I have kept going this way, anyway? I wondered. Maybe getting fired was for the best. I hated it there but made too much money to quit, so I was stuck, and I knew it. My golden handcuffs had been removed.

At first, I was able to summon some excitement for a fresh start. But after a couple of months, as our meager savings depleted, I had no choice but to accept a job at another firm. This one came with a long commute and a pay cut—but I told myself it was better than nothing. But our financial distress worsened, and we fell deeper into debt. The worse things got, the less I liked myself. I had lost my purpose, passion, and joy. I had fallen out of love with my profession and felt rudderless.

This new firm represented insurance companies, and I hated the work. I wrote reservation of rights letters and defended carriers in bad faith lawsuits. The purpose of my job was to help insurance companies avoid their coverage obligations. I was demoralized because my law license was not being used to help people. Even worse, there wasn't enough work to sustain me, and I sensed another layoff coming. The debt situation had only deteriorated.

I knew I couldn't stomach working at another firm. Should I go back into the restaurant business, where I'd worked before law school? Managing a kitchen was hard work, but it sounded like a walk in the park compared to what I was facing. But I had to be real with myself: that path wasn't going to solve our financial issues or give me more time with my family.

My intuition was telling me to go out on my own. I sensed there was unlimited potential in working for myself. I craved the freedom to set my own hours and choose my own clients. But I also wondered if my frustration and apathy for the legal profession would follow me into my own practice. I also didn't yet have a client base, and I knew I would be starting from nothing.

Going solo was risky and uncertain. How could I justify leaving a dependable salary when we were already under a mountain of debt?

In the end, I chose to take the risk. I quit my job at the firm and opened my own practice, taking just one client with me.

Immediately after starting my own practice, I discovered something incredible. I didn't actually dislike the practice of law. I just hated working for others. I felt re-energized and invigorated being on my own because I was building my own dream instead of helping others build theirs. I could pick my own clients, set my own rate, and control the legal strategy.

However, I still had many challenges ahead—the biggest of which was that my wife and I decided to divorce. Less than a year into starting my own practice, I was suddenly a single dad, running my business from a desk in the cramped bedroom of my tiny apartment. It was a dark and scary time, but it forced me to grow up and figure things out on my own. I had to become a better dad because those kids needed me more than ever. The kids needed me to lead them, and I first had to learn how to lead myself. I had to compartmentalize the pain from the divorce and separate it from my law practice and parenting. It was a process. I also channeled the pain from the divorce to lose thirty pounds and get in the best shape of my life. I found that I had the best of both worlds as a single dad—I found balance between bachelor time and dad time, and learned to find the joy in both states.

As my practice grew and I eased into my new, complicated life, I found myself feeling grateful for my years in law firms. Not only did I learn how to manage litigation cases, but I also learned how to run an office and how to treat people. (Or, rather, I learned in great detail how *not* to run an office and how *not* to treat people.) By witnessing the worst, I discovered how I could do it better.

Life is about duality. You need to know misery to truly know joy. You need to spend time in the dark to appreciate the light. I learned to treat every experience during the dark times as a lesson, and every moment of the good times as a blessing. The blues visit all of us, but the trick is learning how to shorten the downtimes and pull yourself out. I personally found that productive activity and self-care, coupled with positive self-talk, are powerful antidotes to the dark times we inevitably face.

In the five years since striking out on my own, I have paid off the debt, tripled my salary from my law firm days, and have started building a team. My former wife and I co-parent well, and the kids are well-adjusted and happy. When the kids are with their mom, I've explored traveling and taking my work on the road. I'm also in escrow to buy a home.

I'm grateful every day for this life I've built and, honestly, I'm most grateful for the low points. Without those years in dead-end firms, I would have remained on a path of mediocrity, complacency, and debt. Without the experience of my divorce, I would never have become the father and man I am now. And without that experience of being fired unexpectedly, I would never have rekindled my passion for law and entrepreneurship.

When adversity inevitably visits me in the future, I'll do my best to recognize it as the growth opportunity it is, and remember that it is happening *for* me, not *to* me. I'm now learning to recognize setbacks as growth opportunities in real-time, not years later.

| 9 |

PETER WISHNIE
PERSISTENT AF

IT WAS THE WINTER OF 1964, and when my mother noticed I had trouble breathing, she called the pediatrician, a good friend of ours, Ziggy. He told my mother to put me next to the phone. He heard my wheezing and instructed my mother, "Get in a cab immediately and keep the windows open."

My mother got me dressed as fast as she could and grabbed my three-year-old self to hail a New York City cab. We met Ziggy at Columbia Presbyterian Hospital where he put me into an oxygen tent. That was the treatment for asthma back then. He said everything should be fine, without anticipating that the nurse would forget to turn on the oxygen. I started to turn blue, and that is when Ziggy realized what had happened and turned on the tank. Ziggy later told my mother that, by all accounts, I should have died, but thankfully I didn't.

I would say that was the beginning of my life as a persistent motherfucker.

Throughout my life and career, I have been confronted with many situations that required me to be persistent. I missed forty days of school in fifth grade due to my asthma. My best friend brought me my homework assignments so I wouldn't fall behind. Because of this, I was able to move on to sixth grade on time.

Later in life, I would receive my biggest test in persistence. The first year of podiatry school was really hard. I was able to tackle every class, but when you put six classes of equal difficulty together, I found it to be insurmountable. In matter of fact, so did the school. They told me I had to repeat the first year. I felt ashamed when I had to tell my parents I'd flunked out of school. They were living in Long Island, New York, and I was in school in San Francisco. I must say they took the news well. Their first thought was that maybe living so far away was not a good thing. However, I didn't want to give up on me or the school. I loved living in San Francisco and even though it gets cold there, it is a lot better than the winters in New York.

I had to learn how to block time in my daily schedule and how to study. You see, you go to school from kindergarten to high school and your parents and teachers *tell* you to study, but no one really tells you *how* to study. Once you start college, the whole ball game changes.

In college, as a pre-med student, I took organic chemistry with physics, two difficult classes. However, I threw in History of Rock Music and Beginning Hebrew (I went to Hebrew school for six years). Mixing the easy and hard classes helped me make it through.

The first two years of podiatry school are equivalent to any medical school in the country. Our professors came from University of California, Berkeley, University of San Francisco, and Stanford University. We took two anatomy classes with labs, physiology, microbiology, pharmacology, and biochemistry. You simply can't blow off any of these foundational classes.

After I flunked out—by the way, I prefer the term "had a learning experience"—I went to the library and took out a book on how to study. The first chapter should have been on how to stop looking at pretty girls and stay focused, but instead the book taught valuable methods on how to retain information. My persistence paid off as I graduated, got a desirable residency and fellowship program, opened my practice, and built a successful business that has lasted over thirty-three years.

Persistence was truly necessary during my separation and eventual divorce from my wife of twenty-one years. Alimony almost sent me into bankruptcy. I did well in my practice, though nowhere near what some of these multi-millionaires were making, but my alimony payments could match theirs. Imagine paying $6,000 a week before taxes for two and a half years. In addition, I was paying down an equitable distribution of over a million dollars, putting money into a savings account for my children's college education, and providing child support. The alimony eventually decreased to $4,500 a week for eight and a half years. As you are reading this, these payments are almost at an end.

My persistence played a key role in not only surviving but thriving. During the early stages of my separation, I sometimes had trouble paying my staff, my vendors, and the IRS. Anxiety and anger set in. I couldn't believe the judge would allow this to happen. I was paying my ex-wife more than I made when we were married. My lawyers told me it was based on my potential. I said, "Potential? Potential is something that hasn't happened and there is no guarantee it is going to happen."

I met people who were in the same boat and a lot of them just gave up. "Screw this," they would say. "They can't get blood from a stone." At first, I felt the same way. Then I thought, my best revenge would be growing the practice, paying off all the debt, and showing my ex that no one can get me down or squash my goals, because I am Persistent As Fuck.

Persistent AF is one of the major characteristics of success. People tend to quit way too soon when trying to achieve their goals. The moment there is a roadblock, they just turn around instead of staying the course. Roadblocks test you to see if you truly want to achieve your goal. We get tested daily, and we only pass these tests when we have a true passion and desire to achieve the end goal.

That brings us to another key ingredient for success.

Persistence is important, but success does not happen unless we have a true passion for what we want to achieve. Saying, "It would be nice to make a million dollars" is not the same thing as saying, "I *need* to make a million dollars."

Reaching your goals requires you to have a burning desire to reach them. You know you have the desire if you feel a deep ache in the pit of your stomach every time you think about your goal. That ache is a sign that your goal is something you need to have. It is something that will make a difference in your life and the lives of the people around you. That ache is your passion and is based on your "Why."

To find your why, ask yourself some important questions and drill down to the base answer. If you ask yourself that question for a total of seven times, you truly will find the answer as to why you want to do something.

Here are my seven Whys:

1. *Why is it important for me to pay off the bills?* To have no debt.
2. *Why is it important not to have debt?* To not have stress.
3. *Why is it important not to have stress in my life?* I won't have to worry about money, and I'll have freedom.
4. *Why is it important to have freedom and not worry about money?* I will be able to control my life and do what's important and what *I* want instead of what *other people* want me to do.

5. *Why is it important to have control?* I can help more people and be there for the people I love.

6. *Why is it important to help more people?* It feels good, and it makes me feel worthwhile.

7. *Why is it important to feel worthwhile?* I never want to think small. I want to know that no matter what obstacles come, I can handle them, overcome them, and become a great success. I also want to teach my children not to give up, and to make their dreams big and bigger so they always have choices.

Now when talking about stress, there is a difference between good stress, also known as eustress, and bad stress. Diamonds are formed when stress is applied to coal. There must be stress in your life to make sure you become that diamond. There is a difference between stress and anxiety. At the beginning of my divorce, I had moments of anxiety. With techniques such as breathing exercises, reading positive affirmations, meditation, and the occasional curl-up under the covers and staying in bed all day, I was able to turn anxiety into a "No one can mess with this motherfucker" attitude.

How was I able to go from the "I don't know how to get out of this" stage to the "No one can stop me" stage? The true answer is my why. It *always* starts with your why, and once you have a strong why then you have passion. Meaning, to persist you need passion but first you need the why. In other words, without your why, you won't persist. Like I said before, people stop when things get challenging. We don't think of ways to overcome our obstacles.

There is an amazing book by Ryan Holiday, *The Obstacle Is the Way*, which I highly recommend. If Edison stopped trying to invent the lightbulb every time he failed, we might be living in darkness. Maybe that is not totally true, but we would not know who Thomas Edison was.

The next issue that people get stuck on is the "How." Believe it or not, the how is not that important. What you need to know is your subconscious mind will figure out the how if you stay the course. The reticular activating system of your brain is constantly searching for the answers to the questions you are asking. The better and more specific the question, the better the answer and solution to the problem. Without clarity, the brain just becomes confused, and confusion leads to anxiety.

Anxiety can happen when you are so stuck on a problem that you can't really come up with an answer. The way to overcome this is to take deep breaths and go back to your goals and your why. Therefore, it is important to have written goals that you can refer to often. As a matter of fact, I highly recommend that you read your goals daily. Goals need to be S.M.A.R.T.

"S" stands for specific. What exactly do you want? For example, by December 31 or sooner, my organization will have collected $1 million or more.

"M" stands for measurable. Measurable goals are much easier to achieve than ones that cannot be measured. They allow you to gauge your progress and adjust along the way.

"A" stands for achievable. Goals that aren't achievable will only frustrate you and make it far more likely that you will give up too soon. You need the goal to stretch you, but it needs to be real. For example, you want to lose fifty pounds by Thanksgiving. However, it is the end of September. Is it possible to lose fifty pounds in two months? A stretch goal is losing fifty pounds in four or five months.

"R" stands for risky. Successful people take risks, but these risks are well thought out and calculated. Dream big and take some chances, but make sure you don't commit to something you can't get out of. Say you want to grow your business by 20 percent this year, but you know you'll need more staff to do so. In this case, you shouldn't wait to hire the staff. It takes time to find the right team players and to train them. Hire them immediately, and you will see the growth.

Finally, "T" stands for time-bound. Your goals must have a specific end date, so you keep yourself focused and don't procrastinate. If you don't have an end date, you may never reach your goal. Or it could take much longer than it should.

Michael Hyatt, author of *Free to Focus*, added an E and an R to the SMART goals and devised the S.M.A.R.T.E.R. system.

The "E" stands for exciting. Your goals need to inspire you. Without inspiration, you will not stay motivated.

The second "R" stands for relevant. If you aim to do too much at one time, you'll get overwhelmed. So, evaluate the current demands on your time and understand your values. If you have family or other obligations and your goals don't align with your values, you'll magnify your stress. Make sure all your goals align with one another.

What I want you to know is that, no matter how great the obstacle is, you can achieve high levels of success if you have a big why that you are passionate about, stay the course, be Persistent AF, and enjoy the journey.

| **10** |

LIAT NADLER

BREAKING THE BARRIER

IT WAS A COLD, WINDY DAY in Jerusalem.

The year was 2011, and I was walking with a friend to my next class at the David Yellin College of Education. To the outside observer, it must have seemed like I'd figured it all out. I was an engineer, a mother to a four-year-old son and a two-year-old daughter, and I cared deeply about the educational options for my kids. Since most of the daycare options available at that time served candies, were too loud, and in general were not healthy for young kids, I decided to start a Waldorf school.

One thing led to another, and I found myself pausing my engineering career to go back to school and become a Waldorf educator—which was how I ended up in the cold corridors of David Yellen that Thursday afternoon.

Suddenly, a peculiar feeling spread over my body. I told my friend, "I feel that I need to be in a very faraway place."

She looked at me like I'd lost my mind. "What are you talking about?"

I wasn't able to explain the thoughts and feelings that filled my body at that moment. It was a strange understanding that something big was about to happen, and it was far from where I was standing.

Jerusalem might be the most spiritual city in the world, but not all who are from there know how to fully receive divine inspiration when it strikes. When we arrived at our classroom, I let these feelings go, and didn't give them another thought.

The following Sunday evening, I got my first hint about what my gut had been trying to tell me three days earlier. My husband, Elad, called me on his way back from work to share that his bosses had mentioned a relocation to the Pacific Northwest in the United States.

I don't remember how I replied to this news. I was immersed in trying to figure out if what I was hearing was real—and how odd it was that, only a few days earlier, I had told my friend that I needed to be in a faraway place.

At the end of January 2012, Elad and I visited Portland, Oregon for a week to check things out. We wanted to make sure this next step was the right one for our family.

It was my first time visiting the United States, and it felt so different and foreign. The weather was the exact opposite of everything I was used to and preferred. It was frosty with a light, constant rain. The sky wore several layers of heavy, gray clouds, which hid any clue about where the sun might be located.

Still, something about this place felt right to me. I knew it was exactly where we needed to be in the next phase of our lives.

In June, all four of us landed in Portland. My kids looked around in wonder. I was also excited, and more than a little scared.

How do you start fresh in a place where you don't culturally belong, don't understand the language, and are without any friends or family around you? It was culture shock at its best, and it challenged us in more ways than we could have possibly anticipated.

Everything was different from what we knew—even the social life. Back in Israel, I could meet the parents of my kids' friends from daycare and, even without extensive planning or knowing each other very well, we could find ourselves having a long afternoon playdate that included dinner. Here, every playdate had to be arranged days, if not weeks, ahead of time, and often didn't include any food. Not even a snack. It seemed very cold and weird at the beginning, but eventually, I adjusted and even came to appreciate the boundaries.

And then, there was the food.

Every trip to the supermarket took us hours. We needed to learn where everything was located, decipher the names on the packages, and learn what each ingredient meant. It was incredibly difficult to find whole, sugar-free food options, particularly for the kids.

Those first couple of years were mostly dedicated to acclimation. The kids picked up English very quickly, and within a few months were completely fluent. Soon, they couldn't remember a time when they didn't know a single word of the language. For me, it was much harder. Creating new friendships was a job on its own.

In our third year, I was finally able to get a job. Until then, I hadn't legally been allowed to work. When I finally did get my permit, my initial thought was to apply to high-tech companies as an engineer or project manager—but very quickly, something changed my mind.

You see, in 2008, my family and I made a huge change in our diet. We eliminated processed foods and sugar, and started eating nutritious, plant-based whole foods that nourished our bodies. We went from fatigued, anemic, and unhealthy to energetic, strong, and vibrant.

To the average person, this could have been another dietary change, but for me, this was the beginning of everything. Prior to this change, I had not been able to perform. I would wake up in the morning with a list of tasks to do and things to accomplish—and then, right after breakfast, I would feel like the only thing I could do was lie down and rest. I can't even describe how difficult and sad this was. It was like I couldn't really live my life.

When we shifted our diet and my energy increased, my migraines and body aches went away. I felt like I could finally start living again! Naturally, I was eager to learn more about the connection between diet and health, so I dove into research, trying to understand the effects of food on the human body, and developing recipes to meet our taste buds without risking our health.

Back to Portland, circa 2015 …

My life at that point revolved around the kids, cooking, hosting, working out, dancing, and creating new friendships. One day, while having lunch with a friend, we talked deeply about food, veganism, and the science behind plant-based eating. Then, I shared that I was pursuing a job in my former field. "What is the best approach to getting hired by a big tech company?" I asked.

"Liat," she replied. "Why would you do that? You're not an engineer. You're a nutritionist!"

This really upset me. How dare she? There aren't many female engineers in the tech world, and it took me a lot of time and dedication to become one. How could she tell me that I'm not an engineer?

Two weeks passed. I let her words echo in my head. And, at the end of those two weeks, I realized that she was right.

Ever since I'd changed my life and health through diet, I'd spent so much time researching, trying to understand the science behind food, developing new recipes, and talking about nutrition at every opportunity. People already asked me for my advice all the time, and I loved helping them. So, why not make a career out of it?

However, if I was going to give anyone professional advice,

it should be based on reliable knowledge—which meant earning a degree in nutrition. And so began my American college experience.

Getting into a nutrition program wasn't easy. I'll spare you the details about all of the bureaucratic hoops I had to jump through as an international student, the prerequisite courses I had to complete, and the job I had to take to make sure this adventure wouldn't affect my family financially. Because while those were frustrating, they were nowhere near the biggest hurdle for me.

My biggest challenge, by far, was the language barrier.

In order to succeed, I needed to learn how to communicate formally and informally in English. Even after three years of living in an English-speaking country, my language skills were very basic. Even a simple text message or email took me a long time to formulate. Now, I was being asked to write articles and do assignments at a collegiate level.

No matter how advanced my knowledge was in each class, or how much time I dedicated to creating the most holistic solutions for my assignments, I always received negative feedback about my English. I was even asked to send my assignments for review by an editor before submitting them because my language "wasn't professional enough."

Don't think I didn't appreciate the feedback. I did. If there is anything I like it's the opportunity to grow and evolve. However, there wasn't a lot I could do in this situation to make things better. I had to submit between eight and eleven written assignments every week, all while working and taking care of our two young kids. In addition, I was training for my black belt in Taekwondo. I had no time or financial ability to send my assignments for review before submission.

By the time I finally graduated, my English had become a serious point of discomfort for me. I was concerned that no one would want to work with me because of my accent. All the criticism I received in school had convinced me that I wasn't good enough to be a top professional in my field—that I would never be able to make it.

But life had other plans for me.

In July 2017, I officially founded my nutrition business. For a long time, I avoided making videos and creating content because I was afraid it wouldn't be professional enough. Once, I called a client who had been referred to me by her doctor. After introducing myself and stating the reason for my call, the woman yelled at me, "I can't understand a word you're saying with that accent!"

I know I have an accent, I thought to myself, *but it's not something I can change easily.* I was (and still am) constantly striving to learn and grow. My sadness in that moment wasn't about needing everyone to understand me or give me special treatment. I knew that my communication was my responsibility. I was doing my best. And yet, I couldn't do my best work for this client because my English wasn't perfect.

This only encouraged me to try harder.

I soon found many clients who didn't mind my accent and helped them to change their emotional and physical relationships to food. I love seeing my clients reach whatever dreams they have and find renewed joy in life. Today, I work with local doctors to support their patients, and with other people who find me through word of mouth and my online content. I specialize in helping women heal chronic skin conditions, overcome issues in their food relationships, and increase their confidence. I also have a long list of nutrition graduates who have asked to intern at my practice so they can understand my secrets to success. All of these people have seen results, not because of how well I write or pronounce words, but because my methods provide a foundation for radiant health.

As I love to say, "No matter how 'suck' my English may be, I'm damn good at what I do!"

Last week I received an email from my graduate program mentor:

> *Hi Liat! I am reaching out as your name has come up multiple times from students researching nutrition businesses. As you know, I teach the Business of Nutrition course, and I like to have former students come back and talk to current students about their business experiences. Would you be available and interested in speaking to my current group of students?*

Despite everything I was told, and all my fears around succeeding, I now run the most successful nutrition business in my area.

Looking back at my journey, I realize how many obstacles I had to overcome to get where I am today. There were so many times when everything felt hard, or even impossible, and I was beyond discouraged. However, at no point did it cross my mind to give up. I learned that self-reflection, the drive to grow as a person, and the ability to receive feedback are important, but that feedback is often just one perspective within a much bigger picture. If you know in your bones that you are destined for great things, it's important to take the information and perspectives that help you move forward and leave behind all the other things—most of which, you will find, are limiting beliefs that belong to others and have nothing to do with your capabilities.

If you can embrace that way of approaching life, you will break all the barriers in your way. You will become limitless.

LIMITLESS
PERSPECTIVE

| 11 |

MIKE ISKANDAR
THE TIME
TRAVELER

ACT I

"Ladies and gentlemen, welcome aboard Flight *blah, blah,* heading to *blah, blah,* continuing on to *blah.*"

Okay, I didn't actually say, *blah, blah.* But I might as well have.

Seven years into my career as a flight attendant for a major US airline, I'd made that announcement thousands of times. After a while, the actual flight numbers and destinations became a blur. And, let's face it, *blah, blah* was pretty much all the passengers heard anyway—if they heard me at all over the music in their AirPods.

So, a few years ago, on this particular flight (you know, Flight *blah, blah,* heading to *blah, blah*), I completed my safety demo, did my final cabin walk-through, and sat in my jump seat at the front of the plane. The captain signaled that we were cleared for departure, and moments later, the giant metal tube carrying 143 passengers and five crew members rose into the air.

As our elevation increased, I stared out the window, watching the cars and buildings beneath us shrink to LEGO proportions. It was like zooming out on the world.

I'd done this thousands of times. But that day, something was different. I wasn't just visually zooming out, I began mentally zooming out on my life.

It was August of 2017. I was a few months into age thirty-eight. My career as a flight attendant had served me well, and I was good at it. The service. The cheesy PA announcements. Coexisting with a revolving door of passengers and crew members. Traveling to exciting (and not-so-exciting) destinations.

Is this it? I wondered. *Or is there something more for me in this life?*

Recently, my friend Kim had remarked in passing, "You know, you're almost forty now." Um, excuse me? No way. Not even close. I still had years … okay, months. I had *months* to go before I turned forty.

Gazing out the window at a blanket of clouds, I could finally admit it: I was *almost forty.*

Where did the time go? It felt like only a few years ago

that I'd graduated from college. In fact, I still called myself a "recent grad" every now and then. ("Recent" is a flexible word. Don't judge.)

With that scary number looming on the horizon, I suddenly felt ... like shit.

Statistically speaking, my life was almost half over. And what did I have to show for it? What impact had I made? What legacy would I leave behind? *Here lies Mike Iskandar, dedicated Sprite and pretzel distributor for his beloved airline.*

Over the next few days, I slipped into a funk different from any other I'd been in before.

You see, exploring the world was my cup of tea. I'd worked thousands of flights to hundreds of cities in nearly fifty countries across six continents. But exploring my own inner world? My thoughts and emotions? That type of exploration usually didn't go well.

This time was not going well, either—but instead of melting into a puddle of Netflix and snack binging, I decided to do something about it.

A random Airbnb host once told me about a life-changing experience he'd had at a retreat. I'd tucked the info away in the back of my mind; now, it was bubbling to the surface, ready to be acted upon.

Three weeks later, I was sitting in a room outside of Ontario, California with a dozen other truth seekers. The facilitator welcomed us before listing a lineup of therapy modalities that we would delve into over the coming days: talk therapy, journaling, energy healing, meditation, role-playing, and beating up innocent pillows with a baseball bat were all on the agenda.

It was an emotional, weird, powerful week. Tears, anger, remorse, "A-ha" moments, a blindfolded interpretive dance to Bon Jovi's "It's My Life" ...

Then, it happened.

I was in deep meditation, getting my "om" on, when all of a sudden ... *Bam!* There he was. A crystal-clear vision of a twelve-year-old boy.

Not just any boy. Brown hair, sweet smile, baby face ... this was me at twelve years old. Standing face-to-face with me at age thirty-eight.

"Oh, hey," I said, excitedly. "It's you!"

The feeling clearly was not mutual. This kid's face was full of pain and sadness. He seemed hesitant to approach me. Was he disappointed to see how much hair loss was in his future? (Sorry, kid. I tried everything.)

Then, I dug a bit deeper, and I remembered the negative inner voice I attacked that kid with. "I'm not good enough. I'm not smart enough. I'm not tall or strong enough."

And then, those words you never want to hear from a child: "I. Hate. My. Self."

I felt sick to my stomach. As a twelve-year-old boy, I never talked about it. I never dealt with it. I just silently carried it with me into high school. Into college. Through my relationships. In my jobs. Across the world.

That negative inner voice had never really gone away. Twenty-five years after middle school, I still didn't feel like I was enough. I felt a profound sense of loss, of wasted time I could never get back.

And then, something happened that I couldn't really explain on a conscious level.

I apologized to my younger self. I looked him in the eyes, and said, "I'm so sorry for the way I made you feel. We're gonna do it all again—but this time around, I've got your back."

I walked out of that retreat thinking, "What in the world was that about? What does 'we're gonna do it all again' even mean?"

On the plane back home to Orlando, an idea came to me: what if I really *could* go back to every age of my life? What could I learn about who I was, who I am, and who I want to become? And how might those insights help not only me but also anyone who had a sad little kid inside them?

Failing to find an actual time machine (and yes, I looked), I thought, *What if my time machine could be other people? What better way to connect to myself at age five, twelve, or twenty-five than to have a conversation with someone living and experiencing each of those ages?*

My mission was set. In the year leading up to my fortieth birthday, I would interview forty people from ages one to forty about what it was like to be the age they were.

A couple of days later, I shared this idea with a friend over brunch. She had a very good question: "Why?"

She elaborated. "Is this a strange, midlife crisis kind of thing? Why look back? Why not just move forward with your life?"

But that was the thing: looking back was my path forward. In order to move ahead with my life, I needed to go back to heal, appreciate, and just listen to the younger versions of myself. I needed to stop helplessly asking, "Where did the time go?" and start answering that question, one age at a time.

ACT II

There was only one place to fulfill my mission: my hometown of Durham, North Carolina. More specifically, within the Carolina Friends School community that had nurtured my lost twelve-year-old self. I hopped on the school's website, wondering if anyone remained from my days as a student.

Then … "Henry Walker? No way!"

Nicknamed "The Pun-Master," Henry was one of my favorite middle school teachers. Now approaching his fiftieth year at the school, I knew he was the guy to connect with.

I emailed him a rough description of my idea. His response came almost immediately. "When can you meet?"

As fate would have it, the next layover on my schedule was Raleigh–Durham.

Six months of planning, recruiting, and brainstorming later, I realized something very important. This was not just a project. This was my *life*. So, I ended my lease in Orlando, crammed all my belongings into my Honda Civic, and moved back to my hometown.

My quest to conduct forty interviews began with one-year-old Emery, the daughter of a longtime friend.

When I walked into the house, my friend asked, "How do you want to do this?"

"How does your one-year-old normally do interviews?" I laughed nervously. "Can she even talk?"

We settled into a corner of the kitchen. I squatted in my tiny wooden chair; she climbed up on hers. And what I saw was *wonder.*

She was fascinated with everything: sights, sounds, tastes, textures. And although she got up and walked out on me twelve minutes into the interview, it was clear that there was magic to seeing the world through younger eyes.

In my fourth interview, four-year-old Davey and I sat on a couple of tree stumps outside his preschool. After he told me he could eat a million, zillion waffles, I asked, "What advice do you have for me as I turn forty?"

This little boy looked up at me and said, simply, "I like you."

At first, I just thought this was a sweet kid-ism. But he was the wise one. On this quest for self-compassion, this was exactly what I needed to hear from a younger version of myself.

Six-year-old Reni told me about a secret nest that no one knew about. When I asked her to show it to me, she walked me to the middle of the playground and pointed to an old, beat-up tire.

The jaded, adult voice in my head thought snidely, "That's it? *That's* the secret nest?!"

Then, I watched as she and her friends sat inside this tire, and the six-year-old inside of me woke up and saw the magic.

I learned in those first ten interviews that the secret to a happy life exists in our early childhood qualities. Imagination. Creativity. Curiosity. Playfulness. Resilience. How much of the world's conflict would melt away if we all became our four-year-old selves again?

I'll be honest, I didn't want to move on from that phase of the project. But, just like real life, my journey carried on— and that's when I experienced The Shift.

ACT III

It's Monday morning. I'm slowly approaching the front doors of the middle school that I attended twenty-five years earlier.

My heart is pounding. My stomach is churning. It's like my first day of middle school all over again. All those feelings of self-doubt, anxiety, and insecurity are flooding back.

I don't like it.

I've worked very hard over the past twenty-five years to bury these feelings. To pretend they don't exist.

I don't want to walk back into the school where I was the shortest, scrawniest kid in my class.

Five minutes later, I get myself through the doors and begin my interview with an eleven-year-old sixth grader. This kid has brown hair. Brown eyes. A baby face. A sensitive personality. Basically, he's me at age eleven.

He talks about the stress of homework. Kids teasing each other. His crush turning him down.

And this is all happening inside a classroom where I used to be a student, and where I'd felt the same heartache from my crush turning *me* down.

I feel like I should have some profound advice for him—but I'm right there alongside him, reliving it all.

ACT IV

One of the questions I asked in every interview was, "What is your biggest fear?"

The younger kids told me they were afraid of spiders, monsters, and exploding volcanoes.

The thirteen-year-old said her biggest fear was that the people she liked wouldn't like her back.

The fourteen-year-old I talked to on the tennis court came to me after a loss and said, "I hate my tennis game. I literally hate everything about myself."

Oof. I remembered that pain.

I've seen it since in kids that I've coached, mentored, taught, and interviewed. I've studied the broader epidemic of teen anxiety and depression, and how it carries over decades into all areas of adult life. On this accelerated journey through forty years, it was jarring to relive the transition from the magic of early childhood to the struggles of adolescence.

I kept asking myself, *Why does this happen?*

I got an unexpected clue during my next interview.

A fifteen-year-old sophomore was onstage with other student musicians singing, "Don't Let Me Down" by The

Beatles. Over and over, she sang those four words: "Don't let me dooooooown!"

I thought about myself at fifteen and how I would threaten myself with those same words. *Don't let me down. Don't mess this up. Don't be a failure.* As the weight of expectations got heavier, that voice got louder.

I could hear that voice in the teenagers and young adults I spoke to.

Yes, the teen years and early twenties rekindled excitement, too—from learning to drive, going away to college, traveling, and starting new relationships and jobs. But a pattern had emerged, and I couldn't ignore it.

In all of my interviews, from the middle school years through the thirties, there was a theme of people feeling like they were behind—that they weren't doing or being enough.

The twenty-two-year-old college senior said being "only ordinary" scared him more than the unknown.

The thirty-three-year-old talked about how, once he'd finally checked all the boxes of social expectations—college degree, job, house, wife, baby—life still felt as chaotic as ever, with a whole new set of expectations waiting for him.

When I got to age thirty-five, valuable insight emerged. Suzanne was a writer who shared that her definition of strength was shifting from "hold on for dear life and never give up!" to "just let go." By this, she meant letting go of expectations and the myth that there is some set of external metrics we need to achieve in order to feel peace.

In the homestretch interviews with ages thirty-six through

thirty-nine, I reunited with my brother and my best friends from childhood who had become professionals, spouses, and parents. They showed me that, no matter how much we grow up, there remains a core personality, soul, and childish sense of humor that connects us to our past.

On my fortieth birthday, I became the fortieth and final interview of this project. The people I had interviewed turned the tables and asked me about what it was like to turn forty. With the younger people I'd interviewed and the important elders in my life all present, it was like walking into a room of my past and future selves.

Best birthday party *ever.*

I thought about the words I'd bullied myself with so many times. *You're not good enough, you're not smart enough* ... And it hit me so hard that I would never say those words to the people in this room. And if the people in this room represented the younger and older versions of me, I could never again say those words to myself.

In my closing remarks, I told everyone, "I appreciate you. I love you. I will do anything for you."

I wasn't just talking to them; I was talking to myself.

ACT V

I took an unconventional path to self-compassion. However, this different way of seeing myself gave me a deeper understanding and appreciation for my past, my present, and my future—in other words, my whole self.

This was supposed to be the point when my journey was complete. I figured I'd soak up some of the insights and then get back on track with a more ordinary way of life.

As it turned out, this was only the beginning.

By understanding and appreciating who I was, and am, I gained a new level of understanding and appreciation for whom I wanted to become. I started wondering: what could this process do for others? What if we could all tap into the power of time travel and discover new layers to our existence?

When the brainstorming dust settled, I was left with the blueprint for an experience that would guide others on a time travel journey of their own. An exploration of who they were when they were younger, whom they wanted to become when they're older, and how the power of the past and future could expand and uplift who they are today.

I knew exactly where and how to test this out.

Shortly thereafter, in the very classroom where I was once a student, I became a teacher of eight brave middle school students who signed up for an unusual elective called Time Travel Journeys.

From there, it evolved into a workshop, a summer camp, and a language arts unit that spread to elementary, middle, and high schools across the country.

When a parent approached me and said, "That class you put my kids through? Could you do that for my team of consultants?" the idea expanded into the world of team building.

After a TEDx Talk launched my program on a global platform, I began working with individual adults, counseling groups, and government agencies. Giant conferences have put me onstage in front of two to three thousand attendees—all of whom want to experience their own time travel journeys.

I've come a long way from that jump seat. In fact, I've made a full transition from air travel to time travel.

My mission moving forward is to bring Time Travel Journeys to schools, companies, and organizations across the planet. Why? Because I can't tolerate the idea of another twelve-year-old waiting twenty-eight years to appreciate and love themselves. I won't leave another middle-aged adult without a way to transform self-doubt into self-compassion.

What I have today is not only a new life path but a new life view. For the first time, I can look in the mirror and say four-year-old Davey's powerful words: "I like you. And from this moment on, I've got your back."

| 12 |

JERRY NARANJO
ANGELS WORK OVERTIME

I GREW UP IN northern Colorado, in our trailer home, which was parked on my grandpa's five acres. My grandpa's farm wasn't a farm so much as a homestead, as he lived in a 600-square-foot converted root cellar where he and my grandma raised a family of ten kids.

I'm a wildly rambunctious young kid living what I think is the best life. My dad is working on a broken-down car and drinking beer; I'm sipping on something called The Club, which is basically a tequila sunrise in a can. I am seven years old; Dad is twenty-four.

As the day unfolds, Dad grabs our Honda Enduro 80 dirt bike and tells me we are going for a ride. We travel down dirt roads and head into town. As Dad cuts hard right to navigate an alleyway, he loses control of the motorcycle and we go down in a cloud of dirt and dust.

This isn't the first time I've been in a wreck, but this time is different because, somehow, we found a way to convince each other that it was okay for me to ride on the handlebars.

We were growing up together, my dad and I. Me, too fast, and him even faster.

The angels were watching over us and we got up and walked away from that dirt bike with just a few scratches. But my dad was different after that crash. Maybe he began to understand the responsibility of being a parent. Maybe he just had enough of trading his time for little money. Fourteen-hour days paid for with his body, combined with tough economic times, created an unbearable level of uncertainty for him and he took decisive action. Gone was the drinking, smoking, and wasting his precious units of energy. He became as disciplined in his life as he was on the job site. I watched the transformation happen before my eyes and I smiled. Our angels gave us a chance.

With help from mentors in my community, I went on to graduate high school with thirty-seven other kids in my class from our tiny rural town and gain admission into the prestigious engineering school, Colorado School of Mines (CSM).

During my sophomore year at CSM, a man by the name of Bill Jackson recruited me as a summer intern for Morrison–Knudsen Corporation, a Fortune 500 construction company.

He took me to the international corporate office in Boise, Idaho, and rebuilt me from the ground up. Bill Jackson didn't play, and you were not to embarrass him if he recruited you. He taught me how to tie my tie, polish my shoes, and most hilariously, table manners! See, I grew up eating with a torn piece of tortilla as my spoon and fork for almost every meal! Bill Jackson was an African American Vietnam veteran who broke through so many of his own challenges. He got in my face with brutal honesty, groomed me quickly, and introduced me to an invaluable mentor in John Ajie, who I still lean on today for advice and decision-making.

That summer was the first time I ever flew on a plane of any kind, and it was the company jet. The manager of the mining division told somebody, "We're going to take the kid who's always here early and works into the night." On our flight back from a day of hopping around gold mines in the southwestern US, I was tasked with handing out the Budweisers. I knew from Bill Jackson exactly what to do and how to do it. I belonged on that jet, and Bill Jackson taught me how to act like it. I went on to have a successful six-year career with Morrison–Knudsen after I graduated from college. I spent years abroad living in Germany and Venezuela, as well as a short stint in Australia. I had gone from a small-town kid eating with a piece of tortilla to traveling the world—a transformation for the ages.

I was traveling through Colorado waiting for my next assignment, to be the engineering manager at a bauxite mine in Jamaica. I had reached the pinnacle of my career at twenty-nine, but, as my angels would desire it, the Jamaica deal fell through. After spending some time with my dad, I decided to join him in his concrete business. The decision made no financial sense in any way, shape or form; it didn't even make professional sense, really. But it was the perfect combination of events unfolding just as they needed, to springboard onto a path of major growth and accomplishment. Within three years, we had tripled the size of the company.

The next transformation was changing the name from H&L Concrete to Naranjo Civil Constructors. Why would I use our last name that was so often butchered in pronunciation by non-Spanish speakers, made fun of by most, and did not check any boxes for brand awareness or marketability? Our name generated great pride amongst my family. While we were from beet cellars and migrant workers, our name was everything to us. We could scale this company so large that Naranjo would become a household name and my kids wouldn't have to be so embarrassed to hear people mispronounce it. The name still gets murdered but not as often, and my family takes even more enjoyment from getting Naranjo-branded swag. From New Mexico to Colorado to Nebraska, our family wears our company name proudly, and that more than offsets the mangled "Navajo" or "Navarro Civil" that will occasionally still show up.

In 2018 my dad retired from the business. I was completely in charge of the company at that point. In the first year with me at the helm, we lost a million dollars. I was starting to panic. During the buy-sell process, I worked diligently with my mentor on how to maintain a positive relationship with my dad, so that after our deal was done, we could still be father and son, friends for life. Our relationship was preserved, but the process and the losses left me worn out.

I've learned recently that dealing with emotion and trauma as a man is like a child taking medicine. It tastes horrible and the body can react violently. I reached out again for guidance and this time I had to deal with myself. What was wrong with me? I worked with a mindset guru to release it all. I thought for sure this hocus pocus timeline therapy was a waste of time. And after two days of multiple hour sessions, I was pretty convinced I'd just wasted a lot of time and money. However, over the next few days something had changed in me. I was definitely no longer stuck and my energy to create was free. The transformation was simply this: no man can walk this world without help if they're trying to be the best version of themselves.

Why is therapy stigmatized? Every great athlete has a coach, and most great companies have a board of directors. As men, in small business, how did we ever get to the ill-conceived idea that we are above that? We aren't.

We were rolling as a company and hitting our stride. We landed a large project in the mountains that had an old, abandoned railroad line running through it. It was historic as it dated back to the Gold Rush of the late 1800s. It was an amazing opportunity to deliver a signature Naranjo project, and we did. During construction, I walked the site by myself several times. I was in awe of the beauty and the history of that amazing place.

On one of my walks, I stumbled across a rail spike. I grabbed the spike immediately and knew it would forever live on my desk as a memento of the project, of my pride in our work, and of how we were going to be part of history, building a new river alignment for generations to enjoy.

As I was leaving the site, my superintendent on the project came to see me off, as he always did. He had many years of experience in the river and had put his whole life on hold to come and build this project. As I approached him, I handed him the rail spike, saying in my head, "You were going to put that on your desk!" Although I felt divinely guided to hand him that spike, I remained disappointed that I no longer had the memento.

Months later, as we were celebrating the new river, cutting ribbons, and eating pizza, I approached my superintendent to say thank you. As I turned to walk away, he handed me three rusted railroad spikes. I got the message loud and clear. When you give and it hurts, you get in return, times three in this case.

As I was driving down the mountain to head back home, I took a call from my attorney. I had found a piece of farmland in Loveland, Colorado, that could house materials and equipment for our Denver operations. My attorney was asking me urgently, before I lost cell signal again, to give him a name for the LLC that would hold the farm. I looked at my dash, saw the three rusty spikes, and said, "Three Spikes Farm."

Three Spikes Farm was established. Our company moved over to the farm for a few meetings in the barn, and I noticed how enamored the people of Naranjo were with the two steers

I had put in the corrals. They'd watch them eat, talk about who was going to get what cut when they were butchered, and so on. I grabbed onto that energy and was inspired to bring in seven more steers, so that every senior-level employee of Naranjo would get half a steer by the next Christmas.

Something magical started to happen: we started working the farm for our people at Naranjo, and then for the surrounding community. We teamed up with Colorado State University (CSU) to give inner-city kids access to a real farm. We started a community garden to share the harvest with employees and retired employees of Naranjo. It has grown into a fully operational philanthropic farm, and our next project is a farm-to-table experience for the inner-city kids of the Clara Brown Entrepreneurial Academy in Denver and Billie Martinez Elementary in Greeley. The angels who watched over my education can rest easy now, I got the message.

Our transformation happened organically and with a lot of blessings from above. Our company is led in a heart-centered way with Three Spikes Farm as our cultural touchstone. We're a better company because we give, and we are better leaders because we care. My transformation is ongoing because, once again, I am meeting with mentors and thought leaders to go even higher. It's time that mental health in the workplace is no longer a taboo subject and people can find a safe space to reach out for help. Peace at the workplace can be profitable. Three Spikes will soon hold a men's retreat, or a women-in-construction workshop, or a 4-H group, or more Clara Brown-type visits for young students.

So many powerful people, or angels as I prefer to call them, have been placed in my path at the right time and at the right place. I have too many to thank, but they know who they are. An elementary math teacher, a high school track coach, an MIT-educated calculus professor, a Vietnam vet, the best engineer I know who happens to be from Nigeria, and all of the amazing guides, gurus, and professionals who now occupy my orbit. I hope my story serves as a plentiful bushel of heartfelt thanks to each of them.

| 13 |

JANA ALONSO

THE GIFTS OF ADVERSITY

IT'S MIDNIGHT. I'm eighteen and have been starving myself for the last three years, but today I snap. Today, I lose control. I don't want to be ill anymore, so I eat, to prove to myself I'm fine. If I eat, that means I don't have a problem with food, right? The thing is, once I start, I can't stop, even when my stomach hurts. I eat more in one sitting than I have in the whole year combined. Tacos, flapjacks, caramels, chocolate, pizza. All eaten together within an hour.

My stomach screams at me in pain, as if it has forgotten how to digest. Shame, guilt, and fear engulf my whole body. I don't want to be alive, I don't want to be here, so the only option is to go to sleep. I can't stay awake anymore.

If you have also journeyed through the depths of a mental health crisis, perhaps you too know this feeling: the feeling that simply existing is too painful to bear, the feeling that being in a body is too horrendous to take. You are left with very few options in this state. I went to bed that night feeling only pure desperation. I couldn't see beyond that moment; I only knew I couldn't keep living like this anymore.

The next morning, my system was filled with dread as I awoke to the memory of what I had done, eating everything in sight. Now, while every morning for the last few years I had woken with the dread that I might consume more than the couple of slices of ham and pears I allowed myself, this was different. This dread wasn't only at the thought of living another day, but sheer panic and terror about how many calories I had eaten in one sitting. I was convinced that all that weight had piled onto my tiny body.

The year before that dark-night-of-the-soul moment, I had spent the summer drinking lemonade on the beach because it took my hunger away. If my family offered me any food, I took one bite and threw it away. I was lying every day, "Yes, Mom, I'll grab a sandwich on the beach." Of course, I didn't. I even started hearing voices in my mind telling me how terrible a person I was. I hadn't eaten in weeks, but I had finally shrunk my body so small that I was happy with it. Now, I was ready to die. I remember sitting on a plane after the summer ended, wishing for it to crash so I could die thin, because I knew I couldn't keep living this way.

This wasn't living. I needed help.

This seems like rock bottom, doesn't it? That last night of pain, fear, and desperate binge-eating was the spark, and I decided that I couldn't do it alone anymore. In the morning, though I was filled with trepidation, I found the strength to admit to my boyfriend at the time that something was seriously wrong. Though this was the moment that woke me up, unfortunately there were many more rock-bottom moments to come over the next few months and even years. My awakening was a slow unfolding; not like a flashlight clicking on in the dark, but rather like the sun gradually rising and brightening across the landscape.

The next month was a blur. Every step of the way, I needed strength. I needed strength to allow support and to tell those who loved me what was happening. I needed strength as I researched and made appointments with a different mental health practitioner every single day for a week straight. I needed strength to understand as I was diagnosed with "severe" depression, anxiety, and EDNOS (an Eating Disorder Not Otherwise Specified; basically, I displayed *all* the eating disorder behaviors—always an overachiever here). After that month, my boyfriend and I had come to a semblance of acceptance, but things were about to get much worse.

My boyfriend had booked us a hotel getaway as a treat before I went home for the holidays. That evening, we relaxed in the room, taking a hot shower and putting on those big, fluffy dressing gowns that only the nicest hotels provide. He had told them it was our anniversary, so they brought us a warm cookie, and I gave myself permission to nibble a bit while we snuggled in bed. As I allowed myself to feel the rare blissfulness of a moment of peace, my phone rang, and everything changed.

It was my dad. "I have some news to tell you," he said, and his voice made my whole body freeze up. There was something in his tone, and it wasn't good.

"Mom has got cancer. They say they have caught it early, but she starts chemotherapy soon. We wanted to tell you before you got home."

He may have said something else, but I couldn't hear over my screams of pain. In the movies, you see people scream at bad news, and I always thought it was a little over the top. But I can tell you, at that moment, my body moved on its own. I bawled my eyes out, and my partner held me. All sorts of thoughts bombarded me, some reasonable and others irrational, but mostly I was overcome with an insistent feeling that *things like this don't happen to people like us. This only happens in films. This can't be true.*

When I made it home later that weekend, my parents and I started having conversations about things we had never talked about. I found out that my mother had her first mental breakdown at nineteen (similar to me) and that she had journeyed with depression her whole life, including having her deepest depressive episode when she was pregnant with me. She was put on antidepressants in her third trimester and when the depression subsided after my birth, everyone hoped that I wouldn't be affected by the whole ordeal. My family is notorious for not wanting to talk about things that hurt.

No one spoke of it until I was diagnosed, and we realized that, yes, we were going to have to face it head-on.

In less than a month, I had been diagnosed with three separate mental conditions and my mother had been diagnosed with stage-4 cancer. It would be four more years until I would truly come to terms with my mental health conditions and come off the array of medications I tried. Three years after that, my mom passed away.

When you are diagnosed with a mental health condition in the UK, you have to fill out a checklist that does not ask about habits, behaviors, or lifestyle in any way. You are simply given a diagnosis, prescribed a pill, and told to try it. If it doesn't work you can try another one, and another one, until you find one that fits. If you are lucky, you are put on a waitlist for some kind of cognitive therapy, though you'll be waiting for over a year. And that's it.

The irony was that while going through all this, I was studying psychology at the University of Leeds. There were modules on mental health, and similarly, all they taught were the different mechanisms of drugs used for mental health. We had maybe one lecture on other options, which was basically just a PowerPoint presentation of different cognitive therapies and the percentages of people whom those therapies had worked for.

As I sat in those lecture theaters and doctor's offices, something started passing through my mind. Like a mantra, I thought it all the time:

This is all you've got? This is it?

A pill or a therapy that works on only 30 percent of people? No explanation of *why* neurotransmitters may differ from brain to brain, or *why* mental health conditions are on the rise, or that more people experience anxiety than those who don't? I also wondered why, if you were lucky enough to find a pill that worked, you had to take them forever. Shouldn't you eventually be able to stop taking them and be well? My mother had taken pills since she was a teenager, and every single year for the whole of my life she had a big depressive episode just before the summer as the stress of the year got to be too much. These pills weren't working. My mother wasn't better. That didn't make sense to me. I felt universities were just interested in stats, not the actual humans living with these conditions.

So, as I sat through that not-good-enough presentation on mental health created by academics who were not grounded in actual embodied experience, having already spent three years on various medications, feeling no better than before except for permitting myself to eat a little more, the full deception of the mental health system hit me.

This is not good enough. No wonder we have a mental health epidemic.

I made a choice, then and there, to take my healing and health into my own hands and to burst through the societally imposed limits of how we understand mental health. I decided that I would do what it took, for as long as it took, to become and remain well. Being twenty-one, numb, and not able to feel joy was not the life I would choose for myself any longer. I refused to conform. I refused to give up.

Later that year, I completed my four-year psychology degree with three awards in excellence. In every final exam, I got the highest mark in the whole university. So, you can imagine how shocked my lecturers were when I decided not to pursue anything else in academia. Instead, I bought a one-way flight to Australia, with no greater plan than the feeling that I would figure it out when I got there. I stopped jumping through hoops in order to please others and started making choices for me.

In life we often face a choice: continue doing what those who came before us did and surrender to what already exists, or decide to become brave pioneers, walking a new path in search of something greater, something better.

Graduating depressed and on medication, I felt I was at this exact crossroads. I could follow the normal path, take my medication like a "good girl," keep studying in the conventional systems, get married, have a child, and hope that someday the pain would go away. Or I could use this as an opportunity to go on my own heroine's journey and face the problem with the willingness to find the solution, even if it wasn't mainstream.

Heading to Australia, I chose the latter, and my journey with mental health became my superpower. I learned that healing doesn't just mean getting by. It means thriving and creating a life way beyond what we have been taught is possible.

Why just stop at "well" when there is limitless potential?

Over the next few years, I started studying nutrition, yoga, and meditation. I came off my antidepressants and started experiencing waking up with joy instead of fear. There were multiple depressive episodes on the way, but I came out of all of them stronger than before. When I was twenty-three, I got an email from my mother telling me that her cancer was terminal. I flew back home to become her full-time caregiver.

So, instead of spending my early twenties partying and experimenting, I spent those years face-to-face with my (and our) mortality as humans. I realized that nutrition and practices like yoga and meditation only scratch the surface of health, only offer a tiny fraction of what is possible.

My mother's experience of depression and anxiety heightened, knowing her death was close, but we were able to love each other deeply through this challenging time. My time with my mother—in her womb, as an adolescent, and through her dying and, eventually, death—taught me the truth of health, healing, and living. She was born into a family of refugees from the civil war in Spain. As a child, she experienced a fear that she couldn't process, and that fear got passed down to me. I saw the impact of unprocessed, unhealed, generational trauma on our bodies and lives. I am a firm believer that my mother's illness, mental health, and cancer were a by-product of unhealed trauma and a nervous system always on alert, her death a consequence of a world that doesn't do better with mental health.

My journey with my mother helped me understand the cost of not taking responsibility for our health and the toll of not healing what has been passed down for generations. I decided: this stops with me. If you are alive right now, you have this choice as well. You get to choose to heal and not continue perpetuating cycles of the past.

My journey ended my dependence on any medication and cured my depressive episodes. But perhaps even bigger, it resulted in me creating a unified system of healing that guides anyone willing to take responsibility for their life and healing, to go from small and unhappy to empowered and in touch with their full potential. I shifted my destiny, and now I wanted to help others become masters of their destinies too.

There's a potential within all of us to live something extraordinary, but you have to choose it. That journey may have more twists and turns than you imagine; sometimes it may feel that it gets harder before it gets better, but the ever-unfolding destination is worth it.

Everyone lives, but not everyone makes their time extraordinary. From my experience, the people who choose to see challenges as an opportunity to discover their greatness, who have the courage to walk the path not yet trodden, will indeed be the ones of us who discover they are, in fact, limitless.

| 14 |

JULIA MIKK

THE POWER
OF EASE

I SAT ON THE COUCH feeling completely exhausted, miserable, and in pain. The burnout I'd been experiencing for years now was only getting worse.

Drained, alone, and hopeless, I was stuck on a roller coaster of constant work. I had just finished facilitating another empowerment workshop, and I was so glad I could help many people create a life they absolutely loved. Yet, it always came at the expense of myself—I was dwindling away. I sacrificed my own health as I gave everything I had to others.

Unable to sit up any longer, I lay down on the couch at the workshop venue like an empty sack, feeling utterly spent. In that moment, however, a knowing started to emerge, growing stronger and stronger until it became a loud booming voice from within. It came with an intense feeling of desperation, exhaustion, and power all mixed together, and it was yelling at me:

You cannot do this anymore! No more! No more!

All at once I was hit with an overwhelming intensity and unusual serenity. Like a wise elder, it just knew the truth and was fiercely communicating it to me. There was no BS. No sugarcoating. It was a laser-like quality of instant knowing, a sharp sword cutting through the old fog. The message was loud and clear: *You have to stop this cycle now!* And then the most intense part of all: *If you do not stop what you are doing, you* will *get cancer.*

I received a vivid vision in my mind's eye while hearing this voice tell me what was going to happen next. As if I had traveled several years ahead and it was already happening, my entire body was swept into the experience—the pain, deep suffering, loneliness, regret, *cancer.* It was an intense premonition, a soul-crushing preview of myself suffering a painful death in the not-too-distant future.

Though I knew I was burnt out, I felt that the work I did was necessary. There were glimpses of clarity that the way I was doing this work wasn't healthy, but I felt stuck in it, trapped. For a couple of years, my nervous system and adrenals had been in overdrive and unable to settle. I had traveled the U.S., setting up empowerment workshops, recruiting and training new volunteers in each state, not eating or sleeping properly. Throughout all this, I maintained my private coaching practice as well. It was simply too much for one human to carry. Even after developing bulimia, it still didn't make me understand the severity of the situation. I held onto this almost continuous mantra: *It doesn't matter how I feel as long as I am helping others.* It was martyr syndrome 101. (Seriously.)

Until that moment on the couch, nothing had awoken me from my suffering. Now, I was wide awake, trembling with intensity from the inside out. It was *that* clear. It felt like death and rebirth all at once. I knew-felt-heard-sensed-saw that if I did not stop what I was doing, the next step would definitely be cancer.

So, in that lightning-strike moment of divine intervention, I woke up out of my stuckness, and a whole new resolve arose. A fierce commitment from deep inside: "No! I am *not* going to die miserably!" There was no question about what I had to do next: release the old, heal, and change the trajectory of my future. Whatever it took!

Back home, I looked into what I could immediately stop doing. It was hard, but I released my clients, let go of my students, and stopped my work. I remember one of my students at that time asked me, "Julia, will you come back to teaching and offering your healing work again?"

My answer was clear and simple: "I will come back to whatever my Soul wants to come back to. As long as it is truly aligned with my Soul's greatest mission and it's something that nourishes me every day."

At first, learning how to heal felt like stumbling around in the dark. I had a lifetime of ingrained habits and tendencies to release. What did it even mean to step out of the thinking that it's okay and normal to be miserable? What did it look like to start prioritizing myself? Through work with my mentor and therapist, I began letting go of personal and ancestral conditioning, my attachment to suffering and being the martyr, and my addiction to cortisol—the "high" that continuous stress and hormonal imbalance made me feel.

Of course, on the surface level, nobody could see these issues. Even I bought into my illusion of success. But there was fear controlling my life, and it was holding me back. Just the very act of receiving kindness and skillful support from another human was a major breakthrough at first. I was used to carrying it all alone, and that was a big part of the problem. I had to reframe vulnerability and lean into support.

One day I had an exciting epiphany: What if I let Ease be my employer? What if I did everything that Ease guided me to do? Followed wherever it asked me to go? Choose for myself what it wanted? Instead of my old addictions, traumas, and fears guiding my life, what if Ease took over? It became a fun new motto: Ease is my employer. I wanted it to guide everything I did, said, or moved toward. I started asking myself:

Does this feel easeful, or am I pushing?

Is this nourishing for me, or am I efforting too much?

Is this enjoyable to me, or am I prioritizing only what's best for others?

I gave up my rental in California as I followed the guidance of Ease to Arizona and stayed with friends. They had a big backyard, and I was able to put my tent up there as long as I needed to. What a beautiful gift—they didn't know exactly what was happening with me, they just knew I needed a place to stay. This is where I began to trust that following the guidance of Ease and leaning into support was a good idea.

It wasn't always simple to follow Ease, though. From the emotional trauma of growing up in an alcoholic family in the Soviet Union, I had learned that pushing hard and doing it all without any help was how life worked. It took a full year to step out of this deeply ingrained pattern. It required facing my unresolved traumas and fears and working with mentors and guides to reprogram my subconscious. One of the most important lessons was about the power of Receiving. I had to learn to let in love. Let in goodness. Let in restfulness. Let in support. Let in kindness (my own and other people's).

Another year passed, and I healed from bulimia. This felt miraculous in itself, as I had spent about five years fighting it and nothing had helped. However, the power of Ease and Receiving had changed me on a cellular level. Now I knew what true healing meant, and I knew it in my bones, not just as an intellectual concept from a self-help book. I knew what it meant to receive and fill myself up from the inside out. And I knew how to do it without overeating, overworking, or self-medicating.

One afternoon I was taking in the warm sunshine, as I often did in this new phase of my life, letting it fill my cells with vitality and pleasure, and a desire arose to give and serve again. Unlike the old version where my desire to help others came from a place of pushing and efforting, this came from a place of overflow—I was full and had so much to give. From this place, giving wouldn't drain me, it would only fill me up more. It felt nourishing, exciting, enlivening! The only question was, what was I going to offer? What was my contribution?

At first, an inkling came: *I have important healing gifts to bring to people.* This thought felt good for a moment, yet I brushed it quickly aside, terrified to consider that helping others was the work I had to return to. Being a coach, healer, and therapist still meant burnout in my mind. And burnout equaled cancer. I was not willing to go there again!

So, I prayed and listened for a few more months, until the answers started coming through. It said:

> *Continue to follow the intelligence of Ease. It knows where to guide you. Continue to Receive. When you stay open to receiving kindness, rest, support, and love, you'll pave a very different path forward. A path of purpose and joy. A path of service that is nourishing and rejuvenating for everyone.*

I spent the next two years slowly and carefully paving that path, learning how to take action from this new place within. How do I serve from overflow? How do I create an impact in the world without burning myself out? How do I help clients while also helping myself? How do I love others while fully loving myself? And one of my absolute favorites: how do I receive while giving?

The more I learned this, the more my new chapter came into its full manifestation. I was stepping into my greater purpose, one where I served and uplifted others while being fully served and uplifted myself. I came to the realization that when I prioritize myself, I can be much more helpful to others.

The more I kept prioritizing my own well-being and allowing myself to overflow with health and vitality, the more I knew that there was nothing I couldn't do. There was nothing I couldn't create. Everything was possible because I was tapped deeply and completely into the power of my Soul. I felt limitless, and everything came into a whole new kind of alignment. My healing sessions became more powerful than they had ever been. My clients kept saying that no other therapist, doctor, or counselor had helped them create such a life-changing transformation before. My workshops and leadership trainings took on a whole new level of depth and effectiveness, with people from all over the world being able to benefit from my work on a new level. New resources and opportunities showed up at my doorstep effortlessly. More money than ever before started coming in.

Though it may have appeared on the outside that I was living my greater purpose in a similar way as I had before, now it had a whole new level of power and meaning on the inside. And even more importantly, I could help and empower many more people. Instead of thousands, now I could serve millions because my impact was not capped by my exhaustion and suffering. The ripple effect was huge. I felt humbled, inspired, and amazed—all because I was willing to lean into

Ease. Ease saved my life!

To me, this was real wealth. Real service. Real limitless mission. And even today, I am still on my knees, filled with gratitude and joy that I've found my way here.

| **15** |

KATHLEEN FRIEND

BIRTHING THE INNER ARTIST

IT WAS A TYPICAL WORKDAY. With the click of the doorknob, the clamor of children with pent-up, frenetic energy tumbled into my office and made a beeline for the toys. Mom lagged behind, weighed down with years of worry, clutching multiple bags of provisions that she and her three children might need for the next few hours. She had a tired, desperate look on her face. Her eyes were downcast and her facial expression was lifeless; she mustered her remaining energy to yell in the direction of the kids, "Quiet down and quit arguing over the toys."

She had waited months for this appointment. Child psychiatrists like me are in high demand, and with long stretches between visits. As soon as Mom collapsed into the chair, she launched into a litany of complaints. "He won't listen to me. He is always fighting with his brother. He lies about his homework and the teacher is calling me every week. He needs different medicine. The stuff he is on doesn't work."

On this particular day, the mother's complaints triggered me, and I asked myself why I was spending my life this way. As long as I could remember, there was a tension between my own mother's dream of becoming a doctor and my own dream of becoming a musician. She saw in me the doctor she did not have the opportunity to become, but in my soul I knew I was an artist. My mother could see further down the road than I could at seventeen when I started college, and she wanted me to be able to support myself financially. But my heart had other ideas. The conflict was real and unrelenting, but I resigned myself years ago to working as a physician even though it represented only a small part of how I saw myself.

I refocused my attention back to the present and listened patiently to the mom's concerns. Her words created an atmosphere of heaviness and all I could hear was a long list of "badness," like a rap sheet for a criminal. She was doing exactly what parents were supposed to do: tell me their child's problems so I could offer a solution. I spent years learning exactly that, and it used to make perfect sense. Today, however, it felt wrong and off the mark. I felt more like a police officer than a psychiatrist.

"How are things going for you at school?" I asked, turning my gaze toward her son.

Silence. No eye contact. The toys were more compelling. Or did something else make him reluctant to answer me?

"What do you enjoy at school?"

"Dunno," he said after several grunts.

The initial excitement of playing with new toys faded with his downward stare, hunched shoulders, and frown. I could feel his shame at how his mother described his situation. His eyes hardened as he turned and glared intently at the door. "Can we leave now?"

My heart sank. I wanted children to be seen for their strengths, not their deficiencies. But here I was diagnosing mental health conditions through a lens that diminished the child's uniqueness and complexity, and handing out medicines to match the label. This wasn't how I envisioned things when I went into medicine.

I knew other methods. Drugs rarely served these children well. I eagerly attended countless training sessions that promised non-drug solutions, but I didn't find inspiration until one pivotal conference where I was introduced to a strength-based approach that focused on opening the heart to see greatness. I was so excited to bring these ideas back to my workplace and train my colleagues in this approach.

My enthusiasm didn't carry over to the administrators as I described a vision to uplevel the services we were providing families. They were lukewarm at best. Finally, I got a call from a small start-up school that expressed interest in this

new approach. I was thrilled to have my first training opportunity, but despite my best efforts, they were dissatisfied with
the training and refused to pay me. I was crushed! Not a
promising start to my new direction.

Why was I having so much difficulty inspiring others to
invest in a more holistic approach? I had been successful at
this as a solo entrepreneur in private practice, but I was discovering how hard it was to make changes happen in organizations. At the end of the day, it seemed that people only
wanted my prescription pad. I felt defeated and deficient. How
could my colleagues not understand my vision for improving
the treatment of children and families? It was so obvious we
needed new and improved methods. I felt trapped and mad at
myself for not being able to bring others into my world. It was
my fault. If I was better at this, people would listen.

The boy and his mother left, and the next appointment
arrived. I couldn't continue in the same way. But in that
moment something was unleashed, and I gave myself permission to exercise my creativity despite my seemingly con-
strained psychiatrist role.

I looked at the parents. "We are going to do things differently today."

I told the child to come and sit in the chair next to my
desk with the laser-focused intensity of a bullfighter who
wouldn't take no for an answer. The child moved quietly
without resistance and sat down. Everyone in the room
seemed stunned into silence, yet the atmosphere was charged
with anticipation. I broke the silence, smiled, and chuckled

as I playfully and joyously said, "Wow. You just sat down in my Greatness Chair. I bet you didn't know that!" That simple sentence captured the child's attention and imagination. Surprised, the child came to life and looked around at the chair. Mom and Dad were motionless, watching with curiosity as to my next move.

"I see you checking out the chair. It doesn't look great, does it? Pretty ordinary." The child acknowledged my assessment with a vigorous head nod. "It's not about the chair, it's about the person sitting in the chair. Tell me about your greatness."

Everything shifted. The child and parents relaxed into playful engagement and we had fun discovering his greatness. It was so different from previous appointments. As we weren't focused on problem behaviors, the parents were able to reconnect to all they loved about their son, and he exuded a joyful lightness. When we eventually circled around to tackle the issues which brought them to me in the first place, the heaviness was gone and everyone was on board.

The creation of the Greatness Chair was the beginning of my fully integrated and limitless self. At that moment I knew I had broken through a significant barrier. Deep inside I was an artistic person, and in this one act of creating the Greatness Chair, I finally joined my creative side with my role as a physician. I never believed it was possible. I had been at war between these sides of myself for as long as I could remember.

From my early childhood, I wanted to become a musician. I wanted to attend music school for college but doubted my abilities. When I finally had the courage and opportunity to apply in my forties, I was turned down with a perfunctory, "You are too old." I knew music school had been a long shot but that made it seem completely impossible.

Several years later, I moved my entire family for a job, but I was fired within eight months. Our home was in a remote area with no other immediate job prospects. As luck would have it, during a conversation with a stranger I learned about a nearby college that also had a music school. My heart leapt. The universe had opened up space for me with the loss of my job and I wasn't going to miss this opportunity. I was determined to apply to music school again. I was not aiming to be a professional musician, but something deep in my soul said my life would be incomplete without this experience. Four years later, I had my degree in music and had fulfilled this deep wish of my heart.

My courage and willingness to dive in and take a risk to finally go to music school was fueled by earlier experiences of beating the odds when the path had seemed blocked: I was told I would never get into medical school; I had asthma and couldn't run around the block but became an elite runner at age forty; and I had multiple miscarriages until the birth of my son at age forty-one.

Despite my determination and the ability to follow my heart's desires at multiple junctures throughout my life, there was a further step to unlock my limitlessness. It happened at that moment in my office when I spontaneously created the Greatness Chair to foster a new way of engaging with patients. I finally cracked the code for myself: no one was really holding me back from bringing my creativity into whatever arena I chose, including the medical office. This chasm between doctor and artist was bridged. I felt whole and complete, with permission to create whatever I could envision.

Once I could really see that I was only limited by my own imagination, or lack of it, I started to move into a new field of possibility. In the past, I constantly looked for the right answer, but I had moved into a place of spacious unfoldment without needing to know the specific plan. It felt powerful to follow the breadcrumbs delivered by the guidance within my heart. It was okay to only know my next best step.

The first bread crumb was realizing that my influence was limited if I only saw one family at a time, no matter how positive my work was with the patient. I needed a bigger sphere of influence to have the impact I envisioned. Instead, I wanted to influence my profession and move others toward a strength-based model, one that focused on what was going right, not problems and diagnoses. During meditation, the story of the Greatness Chair came to me, and I wrote my first children's book with that title. I subsequently wrote another children's book, and then one for parents and teachers related to finding greatness. It was so much fun! Suddenly, I had a path to widening my influence.

They say we teach what we need to learn. That was so true in my case! Finally owning my particular fingerprint of greatness allowed my personal transformation to occur. I accepted and embodied my inborn qualities of creativity, relentlessness, vision, intelligence, and optimism. I was never going to second guess my greatness again!

Years ago, my mother told me my artistic dreams would not pay the bills, and I acquiesced to her commonsense wisdom. But the limits my mother (and others) imposed in my life were not the whole truth. I had a say in the matter. Once I saw and owned my unique qualities of greatness, I could move forward with limitless potential.

Coming back to the children, what impact would it have if they could see their greatness early in life? This has become the deepest wish of my heart. I want children to feel good about their unique qualities of greatness while simultaneously developing the inner strength to bring these gifts forward into their lives. I want them to grow up to be the limitless leaders of our future and not lose years to struggle as I did.

I invite you all, no matter what age, to have a seat in your own Greatness Chair.

Here's to our collective greatness growing!

| 16 |

KARI SCHWEAR

WORDS MATTER

"HEY, WHAT TIME are y'all heading over?" my friend Sarah asked.

"Let's say by noon. We'll have all day to party!" I replied with excitement.

Little did I know that this day—July 4, 2016—would be the beginning of the end for me. I was about to experience a breakup that would feel like a death and take months to overcome.

It was a typical summer celebration with an inviting pool, delicious grilled food, fireworks, and of course, tons of alcohol. My husband and I showed up a few minutes past noon, ready to enjoy the day. It started out with the usual crew: me and my husband and two other close couples, until later in the evening when a few more of our neighbors joined in on the fun. When we had these get-togethers, it typically got loud, crazy, and full of laughter.

The big difference this day was my choice of mixing several types of alcoholic beverages. I started with vodka and lemonade, then switched to wine with dinner, and chased it all by downing shots of Tuaca, a potent Mexican liquor.

Not only did I drink too much, but I embarrassed myself by jumping in the pool in just my bra and underwear later in the evening. While that's not *so* bad, I then got out of the pool to change and removed my soaking wet undergarments in front of my friends. Ugh. My husband was mortified with embarrassment for me.

As I stumbled through the door of our home ten or so hours later and made my way past the kitchen, my twenty-two-year-old son was waiting for us. "Wow, Mom ... You are traaashed!" he said in disgust. "How much did you drink tonight?"

Though I don't remember it, out of drunken guilt, I spewed back a barrage of "Fuck you!" and "Fuck off!" among other profanities. All words that should never be spoken to your kid. With my husband's help, I made it to the bedroom and crawled into bed, passing out within seconds.

At the dinner table the following day, my son asked me how I was feeling. "How'd you do today at work, Mom? You were trashed last night, and I'm sure you felt like crap at work, right?"

I answered, "I did okay. Not great. And yes, I did drink too much last night. Was it that obvious?"

He snarkily repeated what I'd said to him. I gulped with embarrassment and burned with shame. His words pierced my soul, and tears began to pour down my cheeks. What kind of mother does that to her child?

I'll tell you.

One who plays the victim card on a daily basis.

One who defines herself as a rebel, troublemaker, outcast.

One who has no self-confidence.

Me.

Kari Schwear.

For the next several weeks, I began researching my options, googling "Am I an alcoholic?" and "How much alcohol is too much?" in the hope of finding solutions to moderate my consumption of wine rather than giving it up forever. That word "forever" felt heavy, hard, and terrifying. It felt as though I was planning a funeral for my closest friend, not just questioning my relationship with alcohol. I stumbled across a YouTube video about the Twelve Steps of Alcoholics Anonymous. The speaker seemed so convincing, yet I wasn't quite sure if I was ready for something like AA. The questions continued in my mind: "Could I really be an alcoholic?"

I spent the next several hours that night drinking, ending when I was halfway through my second bottle of wine around 1.15 a.m. I went to the bathroom, and after washing my hands, I looked at my reflection in the mirror. What I saw staring back at me was the ugliest thing I had ever seen. I had never looked so terrible. I don't know why, but I began berating myself to shreds, saying every bad word that came to mind as I streamed monster-sized tears. "You're so fucking pathetic! You disgusting piece of shit! Look at you! You're gross, fat, ugly, and old! I FUCKING HATE YOU! You're such a *loser!*"

Exhausted, I managed to make my way into bed without waking my husband. I drifted off to sleep, thinking that if I died that night, I'd be okay with it.

I had less than five hours of sleep before waking to my blaring alarm. As my eyes opened, my head felt swollen from the wine and raw emotions, but something was drastically different. I humbly cried out, "God, I'm sorry. I'm sorry for letting you down again. I'm sorry for letting *myself* down. Today is the start of a new life. A life that no longer involves alcohol. I promise." And I've kept that promise ever since.

Although I had a few options, the only avenue that made sense was what I refer to as the "traditional route," so I called a friend who attended regular AA meetings. I asked if she would go with me after work. She jumped at the opportunity, and it was the beginning of a five-month journey of weekly (sometimes daily) meetings, reading the infamous *Big Book*, and walking through the twelve steps with my sponsor.

I listened to the others in the meetings and slowly came to realize that the only thing we had in common was alcohol. It was hard not to compare myself with others, though it was something they preached not to do. Some attendees were court-ordered to be there, some were "old-timers" for whom the program had become a church, and others were so down and out that their situations felt depressing and hard to comprehend. There wasn't much joy to be found, other than an overwhelming feeling of the commonality of understanding, sprinkled with some gratitude. I often felt much worse leaving a meeting than I did walking into it.

Alcoholics Anonymous has helped millions of people, and for that I'm grateful. But for me, it ultimately wasn't a good fit. What it did teach me was to question identity. After all, every time you speak up at a meeting, you begin by saying "Hi, I'm [name], and I am an alcoholic." You're repeatedly affirming and reminding yourself who you are *to the core*. I began to realize that what I said after those two little words, "I am," is my living truth. This is powerful! And I did not identify with the word "alcoholic," not at all. Just saying it pierced my soul like a burning sword. And further, I needed joy in my life. I felt like I was drowning in a sea not only of my own issues but also of everyone else's at those meetings.

As I left AA behind, though, the conflict inside my head was still there. *If I'm not an alcoholic, then who am I?*

Then it hit me.

I am the victim. I am the rebel. I am the bad kid and the troublemaker. I am the hot mess and the attention-seeking people pleaser. But where did these identities come from?

For me, it started when I was seven. My seven-year-old idolized smokers.

Yes, you read that right. I thought it was so cool to smoke

cigarettes. How could I not? Smoking was everywhere in the 1970s. From Marlboro Man billboards to sexy Virginia Slim commercials, to my personal favorite: how to be "Kool" with menthols. So, I did what any rebellious kid would do. I stole a cigarette from Gladys, my mom's friend who lived behind us, snagged a pack of matches, and went off to the woods with my grand prize—my first smoke. As I brought it up to my lips, I smelled it first, inhaling deeply down the length of the cigarette and then back up, as if I was readying to eat a cob of corn. It smelled *so* good to me, intriguing and comforting at the same time. After striking the match and taking my first few drags, I felt like the badass seven-year-old that I knew I was destined to be!

I ran back to the house and swiftly told my mom, "I want to be a cigarette smoker!" But I didn't just tell her, I *declared* it to her! "Declare" is a powerful word, but the intent behind it is even more powerful. I was formally announcing the beginning of my career as a smoker—and though my mom laughed it off, I meant it.

I didn't light up again until I was eleven, but then I was hooked. My identity as a smoker lasted several decades. For me, smoking affirmed my title of rebel, the kid who makes poor choices, gets into fights, drops out of school, and hitch-hikes to a state park to smoke weed with strangers. Those decisions left me wide open to being taken advantage of and allowed me permission to be a victim. I gave this identity power over my life when I chose smoking as a way to fit in, therefore leading to more bad choices, like drinking.

Words matter.

Months after leaving AA, I began working with my first coach, Dr. David, who helped to open up my mind to new possibilities that I never imagined before. He showed me how to eradicate my inner demons and build self-confidence by doing hard things outside my comfort zone. He also gave me permission to love myself, something that I was unconsciously seeking and desperately needed.

Dr. David did something else for me. He planted three seeds for me during our time together that changed the trajectory of my life. He said I would make a great coach, I'd have my own business someday, and that I'd share my story with the world. To which I replied, "No, no, and *hell no!*"

But several months later, I was walking my dog in the neighborhood, listening to a favorite podcast where a guest shared her drinking story. She said something so profound that it stopped me in my tracks. Her words were, "I was a gray-area drinker."

Whaaat? That was me! Her story was my story!

As she described what the term meant—the space between socially drinking and severely abusing alcohol—I knew I had to share this with others. I never felt more liberated than at that moment. The truth resonated with me to the deepest level of my soul.

I wasn't an alcoholic—I was a gray-area drinker!

Once I realized the power of identity and began to own mine, everything shifted. My self-limiting talk and beliefs were a flashing neon sign displaying the ugly truth right in front of me. Once you see it, you can't unsee it. I felt liberated and naked, all at the same time.

Before this realization, I thought I checked all the boxes that meant "success"—nice cars, kids, great husband, beautiful home. But that's not how I felt inside. The cognitive dissonance was enough to drive my less-than-healthy behaviors, like my love affair with wine. The noise in my head became too much to bear, so I hid and self-medicated. Now, I call this internal power struggle "living in the gray"—it's the place where desire meets reality. It's the searching for something intangible that seems nearly impossible to obtain, so instead we stay hidden in mediocrity and complacency, feeling defeated.

Finding a term that aligned with the identity I felt inside revealed what I had been seeking my whole life—purpose and passion to help others. If I poured into others like Dr. David poured into me, I knew I could change my life for the better, along with the lives of so many others. I had a calling, straight from God above.

If believing negative things about myself produced negative outcomes, what if I believed that I was unstoppable? Limitless? Beautiful and worthy? What might begin to happen? I wasn't an alcoholic! I was a gray-area drinker! I wasn't rebellious, I was searching for inner peace. And I wasn't a victim, I was a victor. My apparent mess would soon become my message.

Learning the secret to inner peace and joy begins with a decision. It requires a different narrative and self-talk. And it requires words that truly matter. After all, what we believe about ourselves is what we manifest. Here's what I learned about the importance of what I say, and my core belief regarding identity:

You *get* to decide who you want to be.

When you decide who that is and *feel* as if it's already happened, you *become* that person.

Your identity is what you're most committed to, and this shows up in your behavior. You choose healthy options. You make better decisions. You walk taller and prouder. You have more confidence.

Your new identity will demand you to change (and gracefully so). If you're not growing, you're staying in mediocrity and just existing. That's not living, that's remaining in a gray area—*living in the gray.*

Imagine what it would be like to make a powerful decision for yourself today. What if you looked within to ask what words and declarations you've made that are directly affecting your life? Choose your words wisely. After all, wherever you go, there you are. Be kind to yourself and start speaking power over your life, and you will become truly limitless.

LIMITLESS
LOVE

| 17 |

SARAH LANGE

"NO" IS A COMPLETE ANSWER

I WAS FIVE YEARS OLD when I issued my first Declaration of Independence. I've been at it ever since, and it's saved my life.

Let me back up.

I grew up in a household where there was a lot of drinking and violence. It got ground into my bones. My mother was often drunk. Or on her way there. Or passed out. My first childhood memory is of my father pushing my mother down the stairs. I remember seeing his arms reach out and push her. I witnessed my mother bounce down the stairs, in slo-mo, landing at the bottom in a crumpled, bloody heap. I was two years old.

My father worked long hours as a corporate lawyer. Sometimes, I think he put in extra hours to avoid the shit show at home. When he *was* home, he hid in his study or workshop. Ghost Dad.

When I was little enough to need a chair to reach the stove, I figured out how to make scrambled eggs. I would climb up to the cupboard to get the peanut butter, jelly, and bread. I remember thinking to my small self, *If I don't feed us, we will die.*

Sometimes, my dad would hit my mom. Frequently, my mom would hit us. With my father working long hours, he was never there to protect us.

My father knew what was going on. He knew that my mother had chased us around the house, whipping us with Hot Wheels tracks. That she had come after us with a knife. Driven a screwdriver into my arm. That she had smashed my violin over my head, and a cap gun over my twin brother's.

He knew because we told him.

What did my father say when we told him these horrible things? "Let it go, like water off the back of a duck."

His response left us feeling even more alone, more isolated, worthless—like we didn't matter. Like the abuse didn't matter.

One night, things got so bad that we wrestled my mom to the stairs and handcuffed her to the banister. We fled upstairs, into my older brother's room, and locked the door. My mother begged us to unlock the cuffs, but we didn't dare. Because, not for the first time, we thought she would kill us.

How do you come home to a scene like that and go on pretending that nothing's wrong?

Yet, he did.

We all did.

To the outside world, we were the perfect upper-middle-class suburban family. Nice house. Nice cars. Nice, well-groomed, polite children. Churchgoers. Country club members. Summer homeowners. Everyone told us kids, "Your mother is such a wonderful person!"

How's that for some deep shit irony?

I spent my childhood suffocating under the weight of secrecy, shame, and unlovability. Unlovability? Yes. Because as I saw it, if my mom loved us, she wouldn't have beaten us. And if my dad loved us, he wouldn't have let it happen.

Yet, there was this little fighter inside me. I don't know where she came from, but she's been with me ever since I can remember. She was the one who, at age five, hearing my parents embroiled in yet another fight downstairs, with the sounds of dishes breaking, declared, "I'm *never* going to be like them." That was the moment I drove my staff into the ground. That was the lightning rod that ignited the fire that would set me free.

But the shit show went on until I was twelve years old. That's when my mother went off to rehab. She was gone for eight long months. (Try explaining that to your teachers and friends.) When she finally came home, no one knew what to do or how to act. Least of all her.

You'd think that things would have gotten better when

my mother got sober; at least, that's what I expected. But they only got worse. In fact, my mother's return from rehab was the beginning of the end of our family. Things at home were ugly. For the first few years of her sobriety, my mother was a dry drunk, meaning she no longer drank but still maintained a lot of the same behaviors. Without the alcohol to dilute and wash away her feelings, she let them *all* hang out. All over us.

My parents were embroiled in a toxic, codependent relationship. They were always fighting, but neither one of them was willing to give up the siege. My older brother went off to college, and my twin and I did everything we could to steer clear of the house.

We no longer spent holidays together, unless we were at my grandmother's or aunt's house. I have never felt so lonely as I did when I came home to an empty house on Christmas Eve. (Ho ho ho?)

My parents kept threatening to get divorced but would never follow through. *Please, I beg you, just end the misery for all of us!* No. Such. Luck.

You remember that little fighter I told you about? Well, when I was fourteen, my mother and I were having a screaming match over who knows what. I'm not sure what possessed me to do it, but I hauled back and punched her. In the face! Not my proudest moment, but I was sick of the shit. Her shit. Our shit. It was my way of declaring *enough!* No more bullying. No more abuse! That day, she learned that she could no longer fuck with me, and I learned that I could stand up for myself.

The only thing that kept me sane as a kid was soccer. I started playing when I was five and quickly excelled, playing for elite clubs and teams. Soccer kept me out of the house and provided me with an outlet for all my anger and pain (sanctioned kicking, hurrah!). Looking back, I now realize it was the only place, aside from the classroom, where I was getting any praise, attention, and accolades. Soccer was my salvation.

When I was fifteen, I declared my independence again by joining the boys' high school soccer team. The girls played in the spring, and they weren't very good. The boys' coach didn't want me on his team and took the issue before the school committee. Even though my father was a lawyer, I stood before the committee alone and, shaking in my shoes, defended my right to play. Thank God for Title IX!

It wasn't easy being the only girl on a boys' team, but the guys on my team came to appreciate me. The guys on the other teams and their fathers? Not so much. Still, I didn't let it deter me. If anything, the lewd comments only fueled my determination to kick some serious ass.

Fast forward to college, where I became politically active. From the time I was little, I was the kid who pointed out when things weren't fair, insisted that teachers answer a question they were ignoring, and stuck up for kids being picked on at recess. Yes, I was that kid. It felt natural for me to take my inclinations to the world stage.

As a college student, I protested on behalf of the Sandinistas and for women's rights. I marched in Washington and got arrested for civil disobedience. Back on campus, we built a shanty town on the front lawn of the admissions building. Then, because Upstate New York is cold in January, we took over the building. The next day, we crashed the Trustees' meeting, nearly getting expelled in the process, but convinced them to divest from South Africa.

That was the first time I experienced my own power off the soccer field. The first time I knew that I could—and did— make a difference. I could speak up for and on behalf of those who had no voice. In my role as a rabble-rouser, egg-breaker, truth speaker, and troublemaker, I'd discovered something profound and life-altering.

I started the healing process in college. Even though I was smart, popular, and funny, I was profoundly uncomfortable in my own skin. Without my dysfunctional family around me, I started to feel really sick. Like I'd swallowed toxic sludge and couldn't puke it up.

After reading the book, *Children of Alcoholics* that my mom had given me, I started seeing a therapist. I attended as many as five Twelve Step meetings a week. I could not work hard enough or fast enough to escape the self-loathing.

I was not the easiest client my therapist ever had. I insisted on sitting on the windowsill or the floor. When he cut too close to the bone, I'd tell him to "Fuck off!" But Craig stuck with me, and by the end of my senior year, I was grieving the loss of a mother I'd never had and starting to forgive my father for standing by and letting the shit show continue.

It was through that process that I started to understand the myriad and insidious ways that growing up in an alcoholic home had fucked me up and fucked me up good. I worked hard to recover, and by my junior year I was really stepping into my own, realizing who I truly was, what I wanted, setting boundaries, and learning to say NO.

The fall of my senior year, my parents called me from Philly to say that my twin brother was being discharged from the Army and asked me to fly from Upstate New York to Tacoma, Washington, to pick him up. I told them that if we were doing an intervention, then sure, I'd take a leave of absence and help bring him home. But it turned out they just wanted me to get on a plane and go get him. Um, NO. I'm no longer willing to do your job for you, Mom and Dad!

Later that same fall, I declared that I was staying on campus for Thanksgiving, because I felt like I needed a break from my dysfunctional family, who was having two separate dinners: one at my aunt's and one at my grandmother's. Um, NO, I am *not* choosing sides.

I continued to strengthen my NO. In 1985, when I was living in Boston, my twin brother disappeared from Tacoma, and once again, my parents called me to see if I'd fly out there to look for him. Again, NO. However, I did call a bunch of hospitals, homeless shelters, police stations, and morgues in the area, because I was worried sick about him. Fortunately, he turned up on my grandmother's doorstep on Staten Island a few weeks later—worse for wear, but alive.

Fast forward to the day my son was born—February 19, 1996—when I made a declaration that would prove to be the undoing of my marriage. In that silent hospital room with

Christopher perched on my chest, I whispered into his tiny newborn ear that I was going to work really hard to be the Best Mom Ever. I declared that I would protect him so he wouldn't suffer the way that I had.

In early August 1997, my mother called to tell me she'd found a lump and was going in for a biopsy. I knew it was cancer and that it had spread, because along with being an alcoholic (in recovery), my mother was also a smoker.

I drove from Boston to Philly to be with her the day she saw her oncologist, who told us she had six to twelve months to live. I made as many trips as I could during her final months, desperately trying to squeeze in as much time with my mom as possible, hoping to give my son at least some memories of his Nana. I used the time to say what I needed to say, and to let as much forgiveness and healing happen as possible.

The stress and pain of watching your parent's time wind down is excruciating. It didn't help that I was getting more support at work than I was at home. To my husband, who was an emotionally abusive narcissist (Hello, is Sigmund there?), it was just one big inconvenience, so I started leaving him at home and taking Christopher with me. It was during one of those five-hour car rides that I declared to myself that my marriage was over, and that I would move out as soon as I came out the other side of my mother's illness and death.

My mother died on July 2, 1998. Soon afterward, I told my husband it was over. We sold the house in October, and I moved out on November 11, 1998, taking my precious two-year-old son with me.

In June of 1999, I said NO to the overwhelming stress of trying to juggle work and parenting and left the full-time workforce. I started my own company so I could put parenting first, where it belongs. I've said NO a million times since then, to many, many things.

Most recently, in the wake of my father's death in November 2019, I said NO to putting up with my twin brother's untreated post-traumatic stress disorder (PTSD), which is toxic and destructive. I never know what's going to trigger him. And then, like stepping on a land mine, it's too late. I love myself too much to subject myself to that kind of abuse.

It broke my heart, but also gave me incredible peace of mind. He will always be my brother and I will always love him. I still send him birthday and Christmas presents, and exchange texts at the holidays, or other times he reaches out. But I don't talk to him.

In my journey from being a fearful people pleaser to becoming a powerful Sovereign Queen, here's what I've learned:

To live a healthy, fulfilling life, you're gonna have to say NO and say it more than once. It's going to take a while to retrain the people in your life. When I first started this experiment, I wrote out Sacred YES and Sacred NO lists. What was of vital importance to me? What was I not willing to compromise? These lists helped me set and maintain my boundaries.

NO is a complete sentence. You don't owe an explanation to anyone. If you're uncomfortable about saying no, you can say something like: "That won't work for me/my family." "I'm not available." "Let me think about it." "I'll get back to you." (Then don't.)

When you say NO to someone else, you say *yes* to yourself. You can't give from an empty cup, so be sure to fill yours first. Remember: on the airplane, they tell you to place the oxygen mask over your own face before helping others.

The more you love yourself, the easier it is to say NO.

NO gives you peace of mind.

NO gives you peace of heart.

Sometimes, you have to fake it till you make it. Say NO, even if you're shaking in your shoes. In the early days of NO, I kept waiting for lightning to strike. Guess what? It never did.

The angst is shorter-lived each time you say NO. I'm at the point where I'm accustomed to, and even delight in, disappointing other people, letting them down. Because it means I've chosen to invest in myself, to put myself first. And, after putting my own needs on the back burner for most of my life, this is nothing short of miraculous. My YES and NO are now Sacred Covenants I make with myself.

I have become the transitional character in my own story. I inherited a lineage of chronic disapproval, conditional love, addiction, and violence. I am the person who, in a single generation, changed the entire course of my lineage. I am she who somehow found a way to metabolize the poison and refused to pass it on.

I transmuted the pain of my entire lineage into learning. Growth. Change. Freedom. I broke the mold. I filtered the destructiveness out of my own lineage so that Christopher and all the generations downstream will have a supportive foundation upon which to build healthy, productive lives.

It's not an easy journey, and I wouldn't have made it without the support of friends, therapists, coaches, healers, and the many others who have helped me along the way. And it's been so worth it. I am so worth it. And so are you.

| 18 |

TONI BERGINS

MOVING INTO FLOW

PERFECTIONISM AND "not good enoughness" are implanted into women and girls through culture, society, religion, and families. Based on gender, sexuality, skin color, size, age, ability, and looks, we are categorized into what is expected of us and told what success means. Expectations are constantly piled onto us, passed down through generations, with norms that no longer suit anyone. But alas, this is part of each person's journey, leaving us to wonder: How do I become the real me? How do you become the real you?

I was raised in a Jewish family in New York where the expectations were especially high. The goal handed to me was to become an accelerated student in the "gifted and talented" program. Then I could be recognized as an achiever and pushed forward even more. This, by the way, does not necessarily do wonders for a young mind or nurture positive self-esteem. The pressure to achieve more and more, and to fit into a predefined box of success, meant no one considered me as an individual or considered who I could be. Nor did I.

I internalized the expectations, some spoken, most unspoken, of my father, which he inherited from his father. I inherited the plight of the unlived dream, the "never good enough complex," and the familial head-shaking of disappointment. I internalized the coping mindset of my mother, which she inherited from her mother, of "I'll just suffer silently. I won't make too much noise or ruffle too many feathers." I witnessed one sister who hated herself and her body so much during adolescence that she suffered with suicidal ideation, and another sister who was a rescuer and activist who cared to the point of pain. Needless to say, it was a very emotional family.

All of these voices and behaviors blended with my developing identity, and I emerged with a set of beliefs about the ways of the world: "Success is an unachievable goal to strive for your whole life. Never feel satisfied. Women are to be subservient, moral, and take care of everyone else. Bodies are disgusting and hateful."

Fully conditioned with these messages, I went on a relentless quest of perfectionism and achievement, starting with my body. By the age of nine, I was already obsessed with dieting. I would only eat tuna fish and Melba toast for lunch. All the kids thought I was weird, but I had developed a distorted image of myself and believed in my perfectionist mindset that I was unacceptable.

Next it was academics. I would never allow myself to be anything other than an A student and would obsess about grades to the point I was always anxious. I would come home from school regularly with emotional overload. So how did I manage what I was feeling? I became bulimic and threw up all of my emotions. It became an addiction—a part of me loved the rush of the release and then the calm emptiness that would come over me. When I felt that euphoria, I didn't have to deal with the other emotions or face the traumas and generational beliefs hiding beneath them.

My emotional center felt like seaweed in an ocean of crazy teenage drama.

I didn't know I was an empath, sometimes experiencing and taking on other people's feelings. I didn't know I was clairsentient, receiving constant information through my emotional body. I didn't know I had an incredibly powerful self and massive gifts that would be revealed to me later in life. I shut down anything, including any personal dreams and desires, that kept me from fitting in the approved boxes. I was anything but limitless.

I went to college, as anyone in my box would do. By then I had perfected my body management through bulimia, dieting, and daily gym workouts. I had perfected my intellectual achievement through high grades and academic success. I had expanded my emotional management to include lots of drinking, drugs, and sex. It was all a bit of a blur as I rode the expectation train to the next station—a corporate job in New York City.

New York City turned out to be the perfect place for an exercise-aholic bulimic with addictive coping skills. I was addicted to exercise of all kinds (aerobics, step, martial arts) and had memberships at three gyms. I was at a gym every single day, and often two times a day. This didn't seem excessive to me at the time. I just thought I knew how to pick amazing places to go work out with the best teachers in New York City. The nonstop motion continued into the night when I would go dancing in the clubs. I kept moving to keep from feeling, which was not a great recipe for positive relationships. But after the dysfunctional relationships of my childhood, relationships were my last priority—achievement, the first.

The end of my corporate career came when I allowed myself to admit I was much more of a "rollerblading-while-hanging-off-the-back-of-a-taxi" person than I was a "high heels and power suits" person. While this was the first time I cracked the box of imposed expectations, I was still too conditioned to break out completely. So, I did the next most approved thing: grad school.

While in grad school, I met a guy I really wanted to impress. He was into meditation, so I found a retreat center upstate for a weekend surprise. While he went off to a meditation class, which sounded awful to my movement-loving body, I opted for a dance class.

It was like no other class I'd ever attended. There were no mirrors, no agenda, no equipment, no steps to follow, no rules. There was no way to be perfect! Our only objective was to experience joy in the free expression of our bodies. Joy in my body? Free expression?! The teacher said something like, "Oh, you are all so beautiful." How could I possibly be beautiful in my uncontrolled, imperfect expression?

At the end of class, when we went down to the ground for the final relaxation, I broke open and began crying. I lost myself completely in a puddle in the corner and found myself at the same time. It was the first time I realized I am not just my body and emotions and thoughts. I am so much more. I felt myself as pure energy, my true perfect nature as a soul in this body.

I touched an inner awakening that day. I declared I loved myself too much to continue the incessant perfectionist attacks on myself. I decided to stop going to the gym, treating myself like garbage, starving myself, and doing all the unhealthy things I did to try to control the external conditions of my life. I was on a spiritual journey, and that day was the beginning of my limitless path.

But old mindsets die hard. I pursued my spiritual quest with the same relentless vigor as my past habits. I replaced the gym with vigorous yoga practice. I studied all the forms with all of the most famous teachers in early 90s New York City. I would go to Ninth Street, 11th St., 23rd St., downtown and crosstown—studying Ashtanga, Iyengar, Hatha. I was the model student, perfectly strong and flexible. Handstands, back bends; you name it, I could do it. I loved when the teachers chose me to demonstrate a posture. There I was, right back to trying to prove I was worthy and lovable. But to whom?

Although I had my earlier awakening, I was struggling to integrate the lessons into my life. I was still living in the same apartment, working the same job, connected to the same people. Other than swapping yoga for the gym, I hadn't given myself much of a canvas to do things differently.

One day, I was at the fanciest studio in New York City, a very small boutique with celebrities and the yoga elite. While I was in a forward bend, the famous Yogi laid his body weight on me to push me deeper into the pose and my hamstring made a sound. Hamstrings are not meant to be heard!

I became physically broken. I had been hiding my emotional brokenness for years, and now it had manifested physically. I limped around for almost three months with no yoga practice, and I began to suffer inwardly since I had no external place to dump my emotions.

I decided to seek out a therapist, again. This was not my first experience with therapy. My mother sent me to my first therapist when I was thirteen after I had been sexually assaulted. I saw my next therapist when I was sixteen to help me deal with my bulimia—unsuccessfully. Two other therapists in college were wonderful but benign, just listening silently to whatever I said.

I called this new therapist the "Julie Andrews" of all therapists because she brought everything to life. She practiced gestalt therapy, which allowed me to see my perceived brokenness and wholeness through my own eyes. It was with her that I unpacked the beginnings of my traumatic childhood, the dynamics between my family members, my compartmentalized rage, and my feelings of unworthiness. I found compassion for myself and my past. I saw how I was punishing myself for things I believed were my fault. In one session, the therapist asked me, "Can you feel your butt on the chair?" This was such a pivotal moment for me. I discovered how dissociated and disembodied I truly had been, and how I was staying in perfectionism to avoid feeling. It was like a lightbulb went off in that instant. Bulimia and fierce exercise had been my best attempt at regulating my hypervigilant, overrun nervous system. I knew I had to put myself in an environment where I could heal and thrive.

I left New York City to pursue the healing power of dance from my earlier awakening. Over the next four years, I allowed all those painful emotions—the sadness, the anger, the grief—to come up on the dance floor and be transformed. I healed and forgave my past and my need for perfection. I broke out of the boxes of old limiting beliefs and expectations that had held me back my whole life. I truly came home to my body and found the joy that exists there in my natural expression. I went from shutdown to finding my voice. I found my power and was able to make healthy decisions for myself, not only about my body but also about my relationships, my mission, and so much more. I learned to be fully present with myself and others. I regulated my nervous system and transformed my tension into flow. I integrated my body, mind, heart, and energy. I found my deep connection with Source and spirit. I reconnected to my true desires in life, and I fell in love with myself. All on the dance floor. My empathic gifts and clairsentience came back online for me once I had the emotional bandwidth to handle them and use them for good.

Through my own healing journey, I discovered that I have a gift for leading people in healing and transformation. By combining all of my experiences with psychology, spirituality, and intuition, and weaving that together with the music of movement, I guide others on their own journey from self-abuse to self-love, from stagnation to flow, from fearful to confident, from feeling unworthy to being seen. I call this flow of transformation JourneyDance. It is my true spiritual practice. I have now led over 100,000 people through this healing experience and trained over 1,000 teachers in this transformative modality.

Our ability to heal is what makes us limitless. When I realized I could heal myself from self-hatred, bulimia, trauma … I felt truly limitless for the first time. I knew if it was possible for me to heal, other people can too, and I can help them. I learned to trust myself and realize that I have something completely unique to offer to this world—not what was imposed on me or expected of me, but what is deep inside me and can only come from me.

Sufi poet Rumi wrote, "The wound is where the light enters"—where the gold is formed through alchemy. I created exactly what I needed to heal myself and to transform my wounds into the gold that is now my medicine I offer the world. If you can realize that everything in your life is *leading* you somewhere instead of *taking* you somewhere, you too can pick up your pieces, put them back together in your heart, and find your own unique gold to share.

| **19** |

THE LIMITS
WE CHOOSE

THE SLOW, THUNDEROUS BOOM of the gavel radiated out into the entire courtroom. Its perfectly carved, knobby head with a gold band was the only thing I could see as it relentlessly pounded the courtroom participants into submission.

"Sole custody to the father."

I heard the judge's words, but somehow, I couldn't fathom what they meant. *Sole custody*? How could that be? What happened to the joint custody we talked about? Did I hear that right? I silently begged time to back up. Those couldn't possibly be the words the judge meant to say.

Off in the distance, I heard a woman screaming—no, not screaming, but screeching in anguish. I turned my head to the right to search for her. No one there. Then to the left, but still no one. As I straightened my head back to the center, it washed over me like a slow-moving, muddy river. That's me screeching. That's my anguish. That's my disbelief, fury, and hopelessness. My face was red and stretched, the screech cutting off as I heaved in a breath.

And there he stood, my newly minted ex-husband, dapper in his "I'm a Fortune 50 exec" tailor-fitted suit of dark blue with tiny, shimmering pinstripes and silk Armani tie. The smugness on his face would remain fixed in my mind for many years to come.

That smirk that said, "Fuck you, I won."

That darkness in his eyes that said, "You deserve this."

That shameless, flashing glint that said, "You'll never see them again."

And ironically, that sad, pleading gaze that said, "I never wanted this."

The next morning, a grey sky loomed over my rented house like a haunting messenger of what was to come. His polished Cadillac pulled into the driveway, a black and shiny steed carrying its victorious commander. I had to stay strong, to not let my beautiful children see my utter devastation. It was four hours to their new home in Cincinnati, and with no visitation agreement in place, I felt as though this might truly be my last goodbye.

Through tear-laden eyes, I reached for my daughter, just

over two years old. I hugged her with all my might. My four-year-old son ran to his dad, who prodded him to return to me for one last embrace. I held him as long as he would let me, as he tried to wriggle from my arms. Where we would go from here, I had no idea. But I had lost, and he had won. Plain and simple. And now he would call the shots and I would have to obey—which had never been my strong suit.

I had met him nearly a decade earlier in college. We both had stars in our eyes from the beginning. I mean, he looked exactly like Superman for goodness' sake. But really, I saw him as my Prince Charming, here to save the day, to save me.

In the beginning, I was more than happy to let him call the shots, to have the Catholic wedding he wanted (and his family demanded), though I'm not Catholic. I followed him around from new town to new town as he climbed that elusive corporate ladder. I dutifully hosted dinner parties for an array of his overstuffed colleagues. I basically lived out a traditional 1950s-era marriage, and for the most part, I was happy—enough.

Until I wasn't.

We started growing apart for a multitude of reasons. We were opposites that attracted. I was more of a wild spirit, artsy, stubborn, and unstructured. He was disciplined, corporate, and sarcastic.

I began to feel lost and unanchored, and I wanted something that was mine, something I could control. So, we started having kids, and every insecure, self-admonishing, pre-programmed button I had got pushed, right to my core.

It really wasn't his fault, but the emotional distance between us started almost instantly after our son was born. My little newborn boy cried a lot in those early months; I was never able to soothe him. I would feed him, clothe him, walk around with him, endlessly trying to console him all day while his father was at his "important" corporate job. But miraculously, when his dad came home, all was right with the world. My twelve-hour daily failure would be resolved in less than ten minutes when Daddy arrived, laid his tiny newborn's body across his forearm, and immediately quieted him into a deep sleep.

My reaction to this palpable father-son connection started with gratitude—thank God, my son was finally calm and sleeping!—but quickly I was drowning in self-loathing and resentment. Why wouldn't he sleep for me? Was I a failure as a mother? I stagnated into a heap of anger toward myself, toward my husband, and toward life itself.

By the time I had my second child, a little girl, I was completely checked out of the marriage. I joined a theater group, met a party girl to hang out with, and scandalously started flirting and having affairs. I had gone elsewhere for attention, affection, and validation. During this time, I also applied to go back to school and finish my degree. The day I got the acceptance letter to attend, I sat on the end of my bed reading the words over and over again: *Congratulations—you're in!*

In that moment, I knew I had to make a decision. Stay in a miserable marriage or blow up my entire life and start over. Clearly, I chose to cut the red wire. Detonating that bomb exploded life as I knew it into a million pieces. To my family, it looked like a rash decision to leave my husband. But it had been years of inner turmoil churning inside me until it would no longer be contained, and its revelation would be released to destroy a family, with heartbreaking, long-term effects.

You see, the first twenty-nine years of my life were not filled with an enormous amount of awareness. When I look back on those years—I call them the BMD (Before My Divorce) years—I realize how carefree and basically unconscious I was. I didn't have a real grasp on actively creating my life, or even being involved in it. I was just doing what everyone else in my family had done: go to school, get married, have kids, and now … get divorced. Yep, everyone from my grandparents to my parents to my sisters all got divorced. Three generations worth, and I followed suit.

It was devastating, as divorces often are, and it culminated in me losing my custody battle. I was lost, completely alone, and adrift. But it was then, in that sea of darkness and anguish, that I—the real me—finally began to wake up. I started trekking the trail of a much-needed, life-long journey of self-awareness, forgiveness, and spiritual awakening.

It began with a book. A friend of mine had recommended I read Marianne Williamson's *A Return to Love*, which I devoured from cover to cover. Shortly after relocating to New York City post-divorce, I saw that Williamson herself was giving a talk at the world-famous Town Hall. I bought my ticket, and, as I settled in my seat that night, I could feel a restless, uncomfortable feeling inside. Something big was going to change.

When Williamson gracefully stepped out on the stage, her energy was like a love bomb that exploded over the entire 1,500-seat auditorium. I was instantly in awe, and it felt like a salve for my soul, soothing the wounds from the bomb I had detonated on myself and my family five years before. Just a few minutes into her talk, she quoted the Biblical passage, "I tell you, love thy enemies and pray for those who persecute you." I could feel the tears rolling down my face uncontrollably. I could sense the pain of the battles, the judgment, and the anger of the past—all the years of torment coursing through my body. I began sobbing and continued to sob through her entire talk.

Afterward, I walked home through Times Square in a daze. I didn't even see the bright lights, honking cars, or throngs of camera-laden tourists. Surrounded by tens of thousands of people, I had gone completely inward for the first time in my thirty-four years on the planet. And gradually, with each step, a new awareness began to wash over me. I began to understand that there was a different way to live life.

I realized how disconnected I was, how much I had been living on the surface. I became aware that there was a deeper, richer way of being, of living, of loving. I didn't have to let resentment and anger rule my relationship with my ex or with anyone, including myself. What if I decided to love those I perceived as my enemy? What if I moved into love for my ex, and, more importantly, love and forgiveness for myself? Because surely, I had become my own worst enemy, my hardest critic. There was an unrelenting voice of blame and shame whispering in my ear, and it was all my own doing.

After that, I joined the Sacred Center in the West Village and became a member of their six-person singing group, One Voice. In this warm, inviting, and accepting community, I learned that I was responsible for creating my own life and circumstances—not some shiny prince like in fairy tales or some expectation from society or my family. I wasn't a victim; I was a co-creator. And I had the power within me to create whatever experience I truly wanted! I have never experienced such incredible liberation as when I accepted that truth.

On one ordinary Sunday, during a service at an auditorium on the Upper East Side called the Lighthouse, I walked into the space and noticed an easel on the stage with a large picture of a young Buddhist boy in a burgundy red robe with his head thrown back laughing. It had been taken by one of the Center members and gave off a palpitating joy, which set the tone for the morning.

I sat down in one of the second-row seats of the auditorium, readying myself for an insightful service. The boy, proudly adorning the stage, began to pull at my attention, and I couldn't seem to keep my gaze from him. I have no idea what was happening onstage; songs and words whirled around me as if they were a soundtrack for my experience with this mesmerizing boy in the photo. Suddenly, I heard, softly and lovingly, "It's time to go."

I had heard and felt messages before on this spiritual journey, so I knew this was a true voice from deep inside of me and there was no denying it. I began to squirm in my seat. And, yes, tears began to stream, and I began sobbing uncontrollably, just like at the Town Hall five years earlier. I cried with both sadness and joy; I knew a new chapter was beginning, once again.

It was finally time to be with my children in Cincinnati. I had discovered and healed my connection with myself, and now it was time to heal my relationship with my kids—and my ex.

I rented a cute two-bedroom apartment in a trendy little neighborhood in Cincinnati, about twenty minutes from where the kids were living with their father, his wife, and their three other children. I set up a meeting with my ex to work out the details of this new living arrangement and discuss a revised visitation schedule.

We met in a quaint coffee shop in my neighborhood and sat in two comfy chairs across from each other. We shared a bit of awkward chit-chat, then a short silence before we began our negotiation. But before that could begin, I knew I had to start with something else.

"Please forgive me," I said. "I know it's been years, and so much has happened, but I want you to know how deeply sorry I am for all the pain and hurt I have caused you."

His eyes began to water slightly. He briefly looked down, then looked back up to my eyes. "I do, Paige. I forgive you."

That was all that needed to be said. We both took a deep breath in a quiet moment of silence. We had come full circle from our wedding day over sixteen years before.

The two most powerful gifts I have ever given myself are, one: forgiving myself and continually striving to forgive others no matter what; and two: approaching every setback, challenge, or contradiction to my plans as something that is happening *for* me, not *to* me. I let go of being a victim of my circumstances and moved to a place of empowerment, where I am in command of my own destiny and my own desires.

Since then, I have developed an honest, caring, and loving relationship with both my son and my daughter. I met the man of my dreams after moving back to NYC once the kids went off to college, and together, we have created a life of limitless love, abundance, and adventure.

I make things happen now. I choose what I want to let in, and I choose how I respond to everything—the good and the challenging. I know that I am the one creating my own life. And because I began anew with forgiveness, I opened the door for my life to truly take off.

The only limits we have are the ones we choose for ourselves.

| 20 |

EMILY ESTHER

HOW A THREESOME CHANGED MY LIFE

OF ALL THINGS, I never would have guessed that a threesome would be the experience that shifted my life's entire trajectory.

I met Raya in a hotel conference room in San Diego at a bustling networking event for online coaches and course creators. I was twenty-nine years old and living in my hometown city of New York. After sitting in several Ayahuasca ceremonies, realizing that my fiancé had lost all interest in sleeping with me, and accepting that my life was totally off track, I'd called off my wedding and was due for a fun trip.

When my Head of Sales (and best friend), Evie, invited me to the networking event, it felt like a clear "yes" to distract my broken heart with a spontaneous trip to sunny California. I figured I'd meet some interesting people.

As soon as I met Raya, I realized she was the same woman I'd been hearing about for years back in New York. Long black hair, large breasts (visibly real amongst the multitude of California plastic), a tiny waist, and a devilish smile ... I was intrigued.

"I'm Raya!" she addressed the group. "My mission is world peace, one happy genital at a time!" She was a sex and relationship coach, and traveled the world leading sexuality trainings.

Raya modeled so many of the qualities I yearned to be— feminine, sensual, embodied, confident, and freely expressed. I had worked on myself plenty. I was a yoga teacher and I'd recently completed a silent meditation retreat. I had a successful online coaching business and had just hired my first assistant. But when it came to sex—it felt like a part of me I had barely begun to explore. My sexuality felt a lot like an uncolored page of a coloring book. I'd slept with plenty of people. I'd had several boyfriends and tried dating women. But I sensed there was so much more.

Multiple orgasms? How exactly did those work? Squirting? Is that even real? I wondered.

As I chatted with Raya, I put it together—she was the Raya so many of my male friends had been head over heels for. She was a polyamorous tantrika. A sexually liberated goddess, they told me. Still hurting from my recent breakup, I gazed at her and pondered what she understood about sex that magnetized all these men.

Though Raya's impact on men reached far and wide, there was one man in particular who achieved the status of her primary King. And she wanted me to meet him.

"Babe, I found one that you're gonna love!" she told him over the phone, giggling, as we made our way out of the conference center.

Kevin was a successful CEO of a recruiting company. He had dark hair and eyes, brown skin, and a calm, approachable confidence. He joined Raya and me for dinner at a candlelit Chinese restaurant next door to the hotel.

Over lo mein noodles and General Tso's chicken, we casually broke down the inner workings of their polyamorous relationship. Raya and Kevin had been on and off primary partners for several years. They met in New York at a sex party and eventually moved to San Diego together. Now they lived in a three-bedroom house with separate bedrooms and frequent sleepovers. Both had other lovers, but firmly believed in hierarchical polyamory and being each other's primary. They threw sex parties in their living room quarterly.

And they *loved* having threesomes with beautiful women.

I quickly intuited that I was being courted. That night the three of us cuddled on a furry carpet, listening to music and watching psychedelic art videos on a projector screen. I was enamored with their playful, free lifestyle and began to consider that moving to San Diego might solve all of my problems in one shot.

"What was it like to move all the way out here from New York?" I asked them, with growing intrigue.

"The best decision we've ever made," they told me, stroking each side of my hair.

Hmmm, I thought.

Eight months and one global pandemic later, I left my tiny apartment in Brooklyn and flew back to San Diego on a one-way ticket.

A few months after that, Raya and Kevin invited me over for "dinner and playtime."

I'd never been invited so casually to have sex with a couple I was friends with. Yet there was a grace with which they invited me that felt like an obvious yes. Why not? I was attracted to them both, and I knew I could trust them.

Soaring down the freeway that evening, the buttery sunset melting around me, I was on my way to a hot threesome. The freedom was exhilarating. I felt alive.

What would ensue was so much more than a sexy experience. It was deeply profound and ultimately would change everything.

Raya, Kevin, and I ate dinner and drank red wine. After dinner, they invited me to lounge with them on a splay of carpets and pillows on the ground.

"Are you open to an intentional conversation about sexual health, boundaries, and desires?" they asked me.

"Sure," I replied. It sounded reasonable, and I liked the

clarity and directness they brought to it. What happened next was surprising and delightful.

We each gave full details on sexual health and history. We took turns discussing concerns around the risk of pregnancy. We spoke in depth around our relationship status and desires for both the evening and the long term. Then we discussed "aftercare" needs—how each of us would like to be cared for afterward, should sex take place.

"I don't like when lovers leave without saying goodbye in the morning," Kevin said.

"I want a flirty follow-up text message within twenty-four hours," Raya requested.

The final piece, they explained, was to decide.

Based on everything we'd discussed, did all three of us fully consent and consciously choose to have sex?

Woah.

A lifetime of unconscious sex flashed before my eyes.

Painful weeks of checking my texts hoping to hear from someone I'd hooked up with at a college party.

Late nights after the bar, watching a drunk dude try to put a condom on his half-hard penis without asking me if I wanted to have sex.

Making love with someone I was really into and assuming it meant we'd become exclusive, only to find out afterward he was married.

It all could have been avoided by a simple, courageous, and conscious conversation. The very conversation Raya and Kevin had just taught me. I was blown away.

And this was only the beginning.

The three of us frolicked to the bedroom. We shared fun, sexy, blissful lovemaking, in which I was luckily the center of attention (this was discussed and agreed upon beforehand, of course). When I was moved to tears after orgasming, they asked me to share what was coming up.

I told them, "I've never had sex that felt this healthy. I feel so safe right now. I feel loved. I feel free."

Raya explained that it wasn't a coincidence they'd developed the skill of creating conscious, healing, sexual experiences. Then she invited me to a week-long training where I could learn the same art. It was just three weeks and a flight to Colorado away.

I hesitated momentarily. My company was scaling. We were beyond capacity with clients, and I'd just hired and onboarded several new staff. Could I really take a whole week away and leave my team in charge? It felt risky.

But there was such a strong, visceral sense in me that I *had* to be at that training in Colorado. I barely understood what the training was. The information on the website was vague. Something to do with spirituality, sexuality, and shamanism. My body said, "Be there." I paid the deposit and trusted that everything would work out.

I was a young CEO of a quickly growing company, and I was excited and nervous to leave my team in charge for the first time for a whole week. I thanked them profusely.

The training turned out to be a sort of sexy, spiritual, clothing-optional summer camp for grown-ups. We spent long days in session processing emotions, dancing ecstatically, and practicing tantric exercises. I met a handsome mid-divorce man who instantly became my boyfriend for the week.

On the first day, one of the facilitators, Jose, offered some perspective on what could take place:

"Everything that happens here this week is part of your medicine," he declared. "Including what happens outside of here while you're here. Things may happen this week that will make you want to leave. We ask you not to leave."

And on day three of the training, the morning after a lunar eclipse, something happened that made it extremely difficult for me not to leave.

At breakfast, I was pulled aside by a staff member: "There's an email for you." I had been ignoring my phone and inbox to be fully present at the training.

I read the email. It was from Evie.

Call me immediately. Something has come up and you need to know about it.

I stepped outside to call Evie, a little nervous but mostly calm. I figured there was an issue with a client and that it was probably something the team could have managed without me, and they just needed a little encouragement.

"We received a letter from the clients," Evie told me. "They're unhappy with the services. They're asking for a refund. There are twenty-one signatures."

"Holy fucking shit," I replied. I went pale. It felt as if the ground beneath me was crumbling. This was the absolute worst thing I could imagine happening to my company the week I stepped away from it.

I did the quick math. It was about $50,000 of requested refunds. If I didn't sort this out, we could be out of business almost instantly. I was terrified. And I was hurt. I cared deeply about these clients and had been working hard day and night to deliver incredible services. Where had we gone wrong?

And I remembered Jose's words: "Everything that happens here, including what happens outside of here, is part of your medicine … we ask you not to leave."

I spent the rest of the week doing my best to stay present in the training, and using breaks to make calls to figure out how to save the company from this turmoil. As hard as it was to stay physically at the training, and as much as my teammates begged me to leave, I honored Jose's request and trusted that finishing the training would ultimately serve everyone in my community more than leaving would.

By the end of the week, despite the stress of handling the business conflict, I left feeling like an incredibly powerful new version of myself. Layer after layer of sexual shame and repression had shed. I returned home to San Diego feeling I had fully landed in my body for the very first time. I felt empowered, sexy, and alive.

The next several months were challenging. I had many difficult conversations with clients who were unhappy and requested refunds. While some agreed to repair the relationship and receive free additional services, others threatened to involve lawyers. Eventually, I agreed to a large sum of refunds, which also meant I had to lay off several members of my team. It was one dreadful conversation after the next.

Yet as the clients, teammates, and money slipped away from me, I sensed a growing peace and a mysterious new calling brewing within me.

Though it was devastating to lose everything I'd worked so hard to build, I was also relieved. This business disintegrating meant a blank slate. I could start over. I could be anyone. I could do anything. I could join Raya's mission to create world peace, one happy genital at a time

Over the next year, I surrendered to the mystery as it unfolded. I danced every morning on the beach. I prayed in the ocean. I repeated the sexuality training twice. I met a man, fell in love, and moved north to live in the Redwoods.

I started organizing conscious sex parties. I launched a copywriting service. Squirting *was* real, it turned out. Life didn't look anything like what I thought it would. It was better. I had landed in my body. I was sexually alive. I was creating a new life, guided by my own happy genitals.

Could it be that the mysterious force of the sacred shamanic sexual field casted a magic spell to set me in this new direction? Maybe.

Could it be that a really good threesome changed the entire trajectory of my life? Definitely.

| 21 |

DOMINEY DREW

ALL THE WAY OUT

IN LATE 2011, I paced in my tiny bedroom, alone that afternoon in an apartment I shared with two other women outside of Boston. My roommates were nice, but not soul sisters, and not often at home. The apartment had a sterile feel to it—functional, without much heart. Like most days, I was struggling emotionally, which had pretty much been my default state since my parents divorced when I was seven years old. Struggling within my own mind, always within myself, always against myself.

The cause of the struggle would vary—more often than not, I was creating it myself (subconsciously, of course), rather than having it truly thrust upon me by life itself. But I didn't know that then. I was twenty-seven years old, and nearly a decade into the intensive personal development work I had turned to in a dark moment at nineteen.

I remember it like it was yesterday. "Dark moment" hardly even covers it. I had struggled with depression since my early teens. Deep insecurity, low self-confidence, body dysmorphia, constant negative self-talk, anxiety, and overall self-loathing had become the norm of my inner landscape. I often cried during those years, and I remember the words that frequently came to me were: *I want to go home.*

"I can't explain it, I just … I want to go home," I told my mother one day.

She looked at me, confused, not understanding what I meant. I couldn't explain it further. I knew I was home on our property, in our house, of course, but something inside me, something deeper than I could express or even identify, knew that this was not really my home, knew that my natural state was much more than this human self. Something inside me knew that my real self was much greater, much *more.*

But I was stuck. I couldn't escape the self-talk, the fears, the limits, the *human-ness.* I fought against it, desperate to escape myself, but it only intensified, making me even more distraught.

My mindset grew worse and worse, culminating in a screaming fit of rage, pain, and desperation when I kicked a hole in the wall of my mother's house. She restrained me and, when I was exhausted and spent, put me to bed.

The next morning, she woke me gently, but with urgency. I remember her saying she was sorry to do so, she knew I needed rest, but there was something important that I needed to see. I got out of bed and followed her to the living room where the television was turned to the news channel.

That morning was September 11, 2001.

I was seventeen years old.

The experience of having the violence inside of me seemingly manifested in the outside world was surreal. In the following months, my mother intensified her efforts to help me address my emotional state, and eventually, I found an antidepressant that helped with the symptoms. But no drug solves the underlying problem, and we continued looking for a real, lasting solution.

When I was nineteen, the continuing search led me to a workshop at a nearby retreat center one beautiful Memorial Day weekend. The workshop was a mode of self-actualization work called Pathwork. In three days, I transformed more than I thought humanly possible. My traumas were not yet healed, but suddenly I saw a way that they could be. I was hooked. From that moment, I knew that self-growth, healing, and ultimately enlightenment was my path. Not only to walk, but to teach.

By twenty-seven, when I had rented the sterile apartment in Boston, I was experienced and well educated in the human system, not only the psychological but also the emotional, mental, energetic, and spiritual. I had already overcome so much—many of my insecurities had shifted, from crippling to merely frustrating. My body image issues were vastly improved, although it would be a few years later when I finally cleared enough trauma and limiting beliefs to enter a state of true self-love. The voices in my head were still there, the near-constant conversations and analysis of what others thought of me or what I should have said, but the depression had mostly subsided, and I was off medication.

Even with such significant progress, my inner world was riddled with struggle. Walking around my small bedroom, I replayed in my mind the conversation I'd just had with my mother. Ever since I can remember, my mother and I have been close. Close in a healthy way, yes; and also emotionally enmeshed with each other, to the point where I couldn't tell my emotions from hers, and the idea of disappointing her was tantamount to death. Since her divorce from my father when I was seven, I had taken on a parental role that ensured my survival, in my child mind, and we just … never stopped. Without meaning to, I had taken on responsibility for her emotional well-being, making sure she was okay enough through the divorce to take care of me. As an adult, I found myself deeply conflicted: torn in two by my authentic desire to express who I am, and my compulsive, distorted need to make others happy by people pleasing and needing others to validate and approve of me. The tale of my struggle was as old as I was, creating yet another mental trap to overcome.

In my mid-twenties, during the early years of my intensive growth, I attended a four-year energy healing school. One day, as I sat in class listening to the teacher at the front of the room, one of my fellow students raised her hand and asked if she could go to the bathroom. The teacher looked at her squarely and said, "Well, they're your feet, aren't they?"

My world rocked. Wait, *what?* Never in my life had I considered this; never had I consciously realized it. My mind whirled.

They *are?*

I felt the template of my previous way of thinking shift and change. They *are* my feet! They will take me wherever I want them to, and only where I want them to. The implications of this new freedom hit me like a wave, as I considered this new way of seeing myself and the world. The revolutionary nature of this realization lent perspective to how restricted I had kept myself.

I needed someone to give me permission even to use my own feet.

Years later, in my sterile apartment in Boston, I paced across my small bedroom. I wore clothes that were comfortable, but not attractive. I still felt uncomfortable in my physical body, which made finding clothes I felt good in nearly impossible. I paced in my room and felt the way I'd felt since I was a teenager—trapped.

I was trapped in a physical body I didn't like, trapped in my mind, trapped between the desire to be myself and the death that on some level I was sure would come if I truly risked it. I wanted, desperately longed, to be free, to be myself—but I couldn't. More than anything else, I still felt trapped in this realm, in this world, in the ego. And when that trapped feeling got bad enough, I wanted out.

All the way out.

I had felt the desire to die since I was fifteen years old. Not consistently, but periodically—and powerfully. Walking around the small room, overanalyzing the conversation with my mother, feeling trapped between being me and caretaking her, I felt it again.

That powerful desire to exit, to leave it all behind. Death seemed a small price to pay for relief from this feeling of being trapped. I felt the urge build. I wanted to scream, to explode, to escape!

And then suddenly, I had an idea.

Something in that moment was different from the thousands of times I had felt it before. In that moment, there was a voice—a voice I had never heard before.

Why don't you just leave?

Wait, what?

Well, look, the voice said, as a new awareness stole over me and I processed what it was saying—not a disembodied voice, but a new perspective of my own. *You're wanting to kill yourself, anyway, right? That's a pretty permanent thing. People will miss you. Your mother will be far more than just disappointed. If you're willing to risk that, why don't you just pack up your favorite stuff, leave everything else behind, and disappear forever? Total freedom. You could even change your name ...*

In that moment, my entire perspective shifted. Holy shit, that voice was *right!* If things were so bad that I was going to kill myself just to avoid uncomfortable feelings, then shit, why not take off and do exactly what I want to do?

Why not be free?

I felt the change in my physical body immediately. I felt lighter. The walls that had been closing in on me became thinner and began to give me space. The feeling of being trapped started to shift. But it was the light that I remember most. Suddenly there was brightening, where the dark had been closing in. Suddenly there was air to breathe, options to consider, room to move. Suddenly, there was *space* ... to be me.

Once the thought had occurred to me, the consideration of where I would go followed naturally, barely a moment later. I remembered a spot I had visited long ago—one that had felt magical, remote, and where I was certain no one would think to look for me.

As all of these powerful shifts took place, one after the other, my perspective began to change. I had an out. I had given myself the one thing I had needed all along: permission. Permission to do what I needed to do for myself. And I had needed something extreme like contemplating suicide to give me the comparison needed to make a shift.

From that moment on, my suicidal thoughts heralded not depression, but a red flag for my system—the place I would reach that says, *You're hurting yourself with this; it's not worth it.* Thoughts of suicide became the catalyst for prioritizing myself, for forgiving myself. From that moment on, my suicidal feelings gave me permission to be free.

Ten years have passed since that day, and through continuing to work on myself I have blossomed, transforming more completely than I could even have imagined at twenty-seven years old. I now have ideal boundaries—firm, yet flexible. I have learned to prioritize and honor myself without force or ego, and I have fallen madly in love with every (yes, *every*) single aspect of myself. From that place, there is nothing from which I desire to escape, for in every moment I consciously choose what I want my life to be. Finally, I am home.

My life is now an effortless flow of joy and authentic expression. While there is still the natural life pulse of expansion-stasis-contraction-stasis, I am at peace in every phase. I now run a successful business teaching other high performers how they can achieve the same.

I have spent years in a state of semi-enlightenment, not only at peace with all that is, but blissfully in love with it. I have learned that the only difference between trapped and free, enlightenment and suffering, is perspective. From the depths of despair, I rose to absolute freedom in a single moment. *Why don't you just leave?* I was gifted the extreme comparison needed to make the shift. In that moment, the shift is just a choice, and every human has the capacity to make that change. It is now my purpose and privilege to travel the world teaching people how to master this within themselves—how to access their true limitless nature.

I have still never told anyone my secret location. And although I have no need for it anymore, it feels like a secret I share only with myself. I like to keep it private, just in case I ever want some time alone.

LIMITLESS
EXPANSION

| 22 |

DANIELLA COTREAU
I AM POSSIBLE

I GREW UP HEARING the word "no" a lot.

I lived with my parents and sister in a very quaint yet small home, so there was not much personal space. I heard my parents struggle and argue a lot about money, and I was often told we could not afford the things I wanted. Eventually, my parents divorced when I was eleven, and my mom worked full-time out of the house.

After that, there was limited space, limited money, limited time, limited affection, and not much room for anything else. Even saddled with these limitations, I had a strong, innate sense that there was way more out there than my current environment allowed. I surrendered to my current circumstances and accepted the situation for the time being. But I made a promise to myself that at some point, when I was out on my own, I would explore what I knew the world had to offer. I held onto that hope, that intuition, feeling that I just needed the space to step out of any fear—mine and anyone else's.

The first time I followed that intuition was at an eighth-grade dance. I was dancing by myself, only a few colored lights flickering. I was in my own world, feeling the music in my body. As I danced, I noticed my body move in ways I had not experienced before. My moves were timed to the music and came really naturally. It seemed like something else was dancing through me, and I felt very free in my expression. I loved how limitless I felt. At that moment, I discovered my natural ability to dance. It filled me up, so I continued to pursue opportunities to learn any kind of dance as I went through high school. I had dance roles in school plays, went to every dance event at school, and spent time at local dance clubs with my closest friends and sister any chance I had. I kept falling more and more in love with it. It gave me a creative outlet to express myself in ways nothing else could. It didn't have an ounce of "no" in it. It felt like a full "yes!"

Eventually, I decided I wanted to major in dance at college. I was full of hope and excitement with what I wanted to do and how much joy it brought me. When I approached my mother with this idea, I was stopped in my tracks. "No!" she said. "You can't major in dance! You can't make money doing that! I will *not* pay for your college education doing that. Pick something else!"

In that instant, I felt my heart break into a million pieces and sink to the floor. I was devastated that I could not do the thing I loved most and that made me feel free and limit-less. My chin dropped to the floor, my body sunk, and I felt deflated and drained of all hope.

Looking back, this was no fault of my mother's. Her intentions were good, as she wanted to make sure I would be successful and able to support myself. Yet, it left a mark of defeat on my heart, reminding me that what brought me joy was impossible if I wanted stability. There was never a conversation with my parents or any family members about choosing something that was my passion, that lit me up from the inside, and trusting that I could find success and abun-dance in that. Instead, I found hopelessness and limitations on what I could do with my life. Of course, they wanted what was best for me, but what my best could be didn't fit into my mom's—or even society's—definition of it. From that point on, I lived with low-grade chronic depression. Sure, I smiled when I needed to, but underneath it all, I was not smiling.

My college experience ended up being me just going through the motions. I had lost any inspiration, hope, dreams, or aspirations. I felt dead inside and kept wondering if this was all there was. I felt numb, checked out, and didn't have direction or a mentor guiding or helping me in any way.

I was completely lost.

Not knowing what else to do, I decided to double major

in French and Exercise Science as I had been studying the language since sixth grade and enjoyed fitness and health and was fascinated by the body. By the time my junior year came at age twenty, I had the option to do that year abroad in France as an exchange student. I felt hesitant and anxious since I had never traveled alone or out of the country before, let alone with a group of other students I didn't know. However, right next to the fear, I felt life start to creep back into my heart again. I wanted to experience more. I wanted to see if there was anything else outside the uninspiring bubble I was currently in, so I tossed the fear aside and said, "Yes!"

My year in France was the first time I went on a journey of self-discovery, exploring my inner terrain, who I was and what I was made of. Since it was my first time out of the United States, the only thing familiar to me was me. While at first I was terrified, having left behind everything that felt stable, everything that I'd been told was the proper path to success, I realized all that had been holding me back. The supportive foundation I'd thought I'd been building was actually propped up by my fear of others' expectations, and it had been hiding the possibilities that the world had to offer.

Now, I had no one around me telling me "no."

I had to make every choice on my own.

I was in a world that was both daunting and totally exciting.

I lived with two different French families for the year and took classes at L'Université De Rouen en Normandie. I asked both my French families to only speak French with me as much as possible as I wanted to become fluent. It was difficult, but I embraced the struggle, knowing this opportunity wouldn't last forever. I visited museums like Le Louvre and went on trips with my French family to their private chateau to immerse myself in the culture as much as I could.

On breaks from school, I traveled around Europe, visiting Italy, Greece, Czechoslovakia, Switzerland, and Amsterdam. I remember standing at the train station in Prague waiting for my train to arrive to take me back to France. It was cold out and getting dark. People were walking past me, speaking languages that I didn't know. I didn't hear a word of English. Nobody knew who I was. I was a foreigner in a foreign land. I had no history there; no one knew a single story about me.

My mind started to doubt and question if I had made the right decision to leave home for a year even though my heart and gut had said, "Yes!" I brushed the fear aside and recommitted to my decision to be there. I would see this all the way through. Then the train pulled up, I got on, and went to my assigned room and bed I would sleep in overnight. I set aside my backpack and laid down, letting out a sigh of relief.

In that moment, despite the immense challenges of being in a foreign environment, I felt free. I began to see opportunity in the discomfort, a chance to explore more of who I was and who I wanted to be. I got excited at the idea that I could create or recreate myself in any way I chose. Every country and language became another new experience that stretched me outside of my comfort zone more and more. By seeing and participating in all these different cultures and environments, I saw worlds of possibility in front of me at every turn!

Then something even bigger happened.

About halfway through my year abroad, one evening I turned in early. I needed a break from all the travel and social activities to be alone to integrate and process my experiences. I was laying on my bed with headphones on, listening to Enya, one of my favorite musicians at the time. I was pulled into an altered state partially by the fatigue I felt and partially by letting myself be carried by the music. It was during this spontaneous meditation that I met my own soul.

I could see the shape of my human form, but it was transparent and luminescent. Immediately, I felt relief, gratitude, and overwhelming love as tears ran from my eyes. My body was still to the point where I couldn't feel it anymore. The best way I can describe it is that I was seeing and feeling the energy of my soul. It confirmed something I knew deep down but wasn't able to discover until that moment. I was overcome by extreme relief and gratitude, knowing that the truth of my inner identity was being revealed. I felt an incredible sense of love and limitlessness with more infinite possibilities. I was in a space that had no borders, no boundaries, and no linear time, yet I was aware that I was part of that space too. I was present, but I also felt something so much greater than me.

I remained in this state for at least an hour. Though I wanted to stay in this energy forever because I felt so much peace, eventually I drifted back into my body and my eyes opened. I was in awe of what I had just experienced. No drugs,

no near-death experience, but I had gone through a spontaneous and profound meeting. I knew I would never forget it. I
suddenly had new eyes through which I saw the world. It was
not limited to my body, nor to living on this earth.

I made a commitment to remember and take the experience with me. I knew it didn't have to end. My body felt different, and I let it sink in. Inside me, a door had opened, and
I was filled with a spiritual hunger, sensing the possibilities
within myself and wanting to know more. From that inward
journey on my bed that night, I got to see that there is more to
me than meets the eye. I saw a world of possibility within.

By the end of the year, I was a completely different person
in the best way. I felt a shift and was more fully myself. That
year allowed me the space to explore different worlds, ideas,
people, ways of life, languages, and cultures, each giving me
a different perspective on myself. My love of languages deep-
ened. My eyes, heart, and mind were opened to experiences
outside of the regular day-to-day routines back at home. The
trip also awakened my love of travel, and I learned that it was
something that truly fed my soul.

Coming back home for my senior year, I had a completely
new outlook. I changed my location on campus to hang out
with more spiritual folks. That spiritual hunger drove me
into books and conversations with people who were having
similar experiences. What I wanted to wear changed, and
what I ate changed. That final year in college, I felt happier
with who I was and with my life. I wasn't on autopilot anymore, drifting and depressed, just going through the motions.

I understood that there were unlimited possibilities for my life. I felt better, became healthier, and fell in love with a young man that matched it all. Everything began to be more aligned and truer to myself. I learned about the power of changing my environment and putting myself in places that are unfamiliar and new so they can teach me more about myself. I learned that putting myself outside my comfort zone brought me more knowledge, and that the initial fear that held me back was only temporary.

I had fulfilled my promise to myself that I would explore what I intuitively felt from the beginning. This awakening prompted me to continue to follow my heart and intuition, further opening the realm of possibility. Since then, I have traveled to nine countries, moved across the U.S., and created a life and a successful business that is centered around what I am most passionate about and helping others do the same for themselves.

Before, it had felt like what I wanted was impossible, but ever since that first trip abroad, I have been able to see that *I was possible*. My journey was one of learning to listen to that inner voice, the intelligence of my true self, and allowing it to guide the way. This voice is inside all of us, and no matter what sort of limitations others have placed on you—or ones you've placed on yourself—it is there to guide you if you listen. This is the voice that says, *I am possible, I am limitless*.

| 23 |

ADAM BARAZ
21 DAYS IN
THE DARK

IT'S DAY EIGHT of my twenty-one-day retreat, and I'm at my wit's end. I'm sitting huddled on a twin mattress, my flannel sweatpants soaked with sweat. I'm hungry and very tired—yet spasmatic life-force energy is rippling through me, from the core of my body, into the silent blackness of The Dome. There is nothing to do. There is nowhere to go. It's me and my mind—moment to moment to moment.

The most courageous and transformational journey of personal awakening I have experienced was my 2018 journey to Lake Atitlan, Guatemala, to meditate alone in total darkness for twenty-one solitary days.

You may wonder why a healthy, energetic thirty-two-year-old who loves to travel, dance, socialize, and have adventures would embark on such a journey. "Isn't that solitary confinement?" many people have asked me.

The answer is: yes. It's voluntary solitary, with "voluntary" being the operative word. In a passing moment of humor, my mom playfully said, "I'll lock you in the closet for half the price."

I first encountered Darkness Retreat through the teaching and guidance of my somatic meditation teacher, Dr. Reggie Ray. Reggie is a Western teacher who has dedicated his life to translating and teaching the body-centered practices of Tibetan Buddhism, known as the Vajrayana. The Kagyu tradition, which translates into English as the Practicing Lineage , refers to a 1,000-plus-year-old tradition of Indian–Tibetan meditation masters. Spiritual icons, such as the Yogi Milarepa, who essentially devoted his entire life to meditating in the mountains, literally practicing his ass off (his bottom had calluses), and eventually gained enlightenment.

Something about this hardcore approach to spirituality spoke deeply and intimately to my Scorpio soul. Listening to a podcast of Reggie being interviewed about his years in dark retreat, I heard him say:

"It's the highest and most stripped down and most naked form of meditation you could ever do ... It's you and it's the darkness, and there's really nothing to do. If you decide that you want to anesthetize yourself by going for a walk, it's not available. If you decide you want to pick up a book and read it, or turn on the TV, or do any of the millions of things we all do to distract ourselves from our own experience and our own life, it's not available."

After hearing and contemplating the simple truth of the darkness situation, a fiery inspiration ignited in the depths of my mind. I realized that, despite growing up in a spiritual family, son of a meditation teacher, having read piles of books on meditation, and spending nearly a year of my life in silent retreat, if I was being honest with myself, I had never fully faced myself. Not in this way. Then and there, beyond the anxious voice of doubt, I recognized that I wanted and needed to experience the extreme sport of darkness retreat.

I journeyed to Guatemala and entered The Dome of the Mahadevi Devi Ashram at sunset, opening the thick wooden door to behold a simple, dimly lit, modern-day cave. The Dome, a mud and straw hut, was a spacious fourteen feet in diameter.

I began folding and putting away my clothes—mentally organizing and memorizing the location of my clothes, water bottle, toiletries, and vital items by the light of a single candle. Looking around from the entrance, the room was comprised of a greenish-gray floor of stone slabs, wooden shelves with space for clothes, a centrally located bunk bed with an adjacent ladder, a small meditation altar, a twin-bed mattress, a toilet, a sink, drinking water tank, and fresh water shower. As the candle quietly burned down, I knew that these precious rays of light would be the last I would see for the next three weeks.

Finally, the moment came and all went black as the candle flickered out. It was a complex mixture of excitement, anxiety, exhaustion, and mystery. More realistically, my animal body just wanted to sleep. Sleep is one of the truly amazing benefits of the Darkness Retreat. It was a unique experience for me to generously allow myself to sleep as much as I wanted. And sleep I did. The first two and half days of my retreat, I entered into deep sleep therapy. Every time I would wake up in the dark, I suddenly remembered that I had nothing to do, nowhere to go, and a (seemingly) infinite amount of time left on this pitch-black roller-coaster ride. Recognizing this truth, I turned my head back to the pillow and plunged back into slumber.

Suddenly, on day three, my body was sufficiently rested and I found myself coming to life. My body was waking up and it wanted to move. This was no ordinary movement. The felt sense inside my body was that I was entering into a sort of waking dream. In a way, it actually felt like my everyday conscious self was going into a winter hibernation. At the same time, the unconscious primal energies of my psyche started coming out to play.

Arpita Kshama-Devi, a radiant Bulgarian woman with brown eyes, Sanskrit tattoos, and a penetrating gaze, was my space-holder. She was my lifeline—my only point of contact with the greater reality beyond The Dome. Though I could not see her, I could sense her. Her presence was constant, steady, and deeply loving.

Every now and then, I would scribble notes to her through

the double-ply slot in the door, about needing a change of sheets or laundry. In truth, it just felt nourishing to be received by the field of her presence. She came by The Dome three times a day to deliver meals—sliding them through the slot in the door in Tupperware boxes, then ringing a high-pitched fairy bell to signify the delivery had been made.

Though the vegan meals were very basic—soaked oats and fruit in the morning, veggies and rice in the afternoon, hot soup and tortillas in the evening—the arrival of food was extremely nourishing to me on all levels. Aside from being my only real form of pleasure, in the form of flavor, another meal essentially meant that time was moving forward.

Early on in the course of my retreat, my mind began churning out deep memories from my life, which began to evolve full throttle into a full-spectrum life review. Many scenes of my youth and teenage years began to unfold.

On one level, it felt very rich to have all this space and time to reflect on and process my life. At some point, however, it began to dawn on me that all this processing was taking a mental toll. I was exhausted from this emotional, deep journey. In fact, I became acutely aware that the swiftly moving trains of thought also produced a corresponding subtle strain of tension throughout my entire body.

On day eight of my retreat, when I opted to forgo the comfort of food and chose to tea-fast for four days, the intensity and challenge of working with my inner world greatly amplified. This experience completely transformed my reality. Suddenly, there was no food delivery to look forward to.

The hours seemed to stretch out infinitely longer. I was very light-headed and my body was pouring out sweat.

The first eight days felt like an eternity. At some deep level, I didn't know how I was going to make it thirteen more. Mentally and spiritually speaking, I felt extremely weary. Internally, in my mind, I saw scenes of my close friends dialing into The Dome, calling me on a cosmic cell phone. "Adam!" they would say. "We're all going out to a great party tonight! Wanna join us?"

Hearing their cheerful voices, I felt myself nearly leaping out of my skin with FOMO (Fear of Missing Out). I would quietly reply to them, "Ah, it's okay, just go on without me. I'll be here."

… moment to moment to moment.

While contemplating eternity during one afternoon session, an insight dawned in my mind. In a way I had never fully acknowledged before, I realized how addicted I was to my own thinking. My thinking mind was in fact the glue which cemented my bodily tension, emotional stress, and unfelt fears and anxieties together. It felt like quite a burden.

Contemplating this, I reflected on my somatic meditation training. I remembered that the quickest and simplest way to dissolve the thinking is to inhabit and redirect my internal attention to the direct experience of sensation flowing through my body. Simply being aware of embodied experience naturally shifts the mind from the effortful state of thinking about life to the natural state of being in the flow of life.

I felt my mind and body gently soften and let go. An inner

sense of spaciousness naturally began to unfold. I felt my breathing open and illuminate the energetic corridor of space along my spine. An upwelling of life force and multicolored flower patterns, similar to a Fourth of July fireworks show, began to burst forth. What my mind assumed to be blackness was teaming with greens, reds, yellows, and whites—a rainbow of multi-spectrum light. It was amazing to behold the display of my inner consciousness. Ecstasy engulfed me. There was a sense of coming home. I felt over the moon with awe and wonder in experiencing the visions that were unfolding.

Day twelve was the true initiation of my retreat. I had a revelation. I had been contemplating the meaning of life, and the meaning of success. Is the meaning of success making a ton of money? Was it to achieve enlightenment? Either way, I felt skeptical, because both answers had a quality of chasing something.

Then, out of nowhere, a childhood memory flashed through my mind—my favorite place as a kid: Camp Winnarainbow. Winnarainbow was a hippie circus camp that sponsored kids of all backgrounds to hone their natural gifts and talents, to learn to radically express themselves, and perform in The Big Show.

I remembered how it felt to be innocent and carefree— just being a kid. Summers at Winnarainbow had a timeless feeling. As the vision unfolded, I remembered a camp song we used to sing:

> *We are the children of Camp Winnarainbow,*
> *We are the ones born into the belly of the beast.*

And if the worldwide struggle was a jigsaw puzzle,
We'd be the ones left holding the very last PEACE.

Recalling this song, I remembered the purity of my inner child. I felt the warmth and friendliness radiating from within. In that moment, I knew my true purpose in this life was to become an adult ambassador, a Rainbow Warrior if you will, of the spirit and ethics of this camp—which upheld the ethos of embracing all people, from all walks of life, feeling the commonality, unity, basic goodness, gifts, and talents of every individual.

As I reflected on the spirit of that place, I felt a luminous sense of courage, warmth, and openness in my heart. I felt a natural, restful sense of freedom within.

The last seven days of the retreat blew my mind. As I connected deeper with myself, and the warmth and goodness of my open heart, I began to feel an energy I can only describe as grace washing through me and moving me from within.

Dazzling white light began pouring through all my energy centers, cascading through my core, emanating and radiating in all directions through the space of The Dome. In fact, The Dome itself began opening and expanding in all directions.

All boundaries and limitations collapsed as the tension, stress, and solidity of my pain, which had riddled my body for my entire life, began dissolving from within. There was an openness of my heart, and a glowing feeling of calm; the only word that captures the frequency I felt in me is God.

What I discovered in this retreat is something that I take with me everywhere, and every day.

The realization that unfolded was a fundamental recognition about the reality of being human.

There is a power, an energy, a force of love in this universe, holding each and every one of us—every moment of every day, through the darkest trials and tribulations of our lives. And though many of us flounder and struggle, sooner or later this force will bring us home to the remembrance of our true selves—guiding us out of the darkness and into the light.

| 24 |

LESLIE GRACE

MODERN MYSTIC

WE WERE GATHERED around the sacred fire, a band of wild mystics tucked away in a lush jungle paradise, increasingly enveloped by a symphony of insects and a comfortable, benevolent darkness. We had been preparing for something I couldn't fathom with my mind, but my heart somehow trusted. When my turn finally came, I knelt at the altar. My heart pounded as the shaman looked deeply into my eyes and then to her bottle of brew. She poured my cup, whispering her secret blessings over it and handing it to me with sweet generosity. I drank swiftly and sat back in my spot, upright with a warrior's stance, and meditated, waiting for God knows what.

How did I even get here? I wondered.

By absolute grace.

A month earlier, I'd left San Diego to venture to Costa Rica for a family vacation. I was twenty-six and had been working in hospice care for several years, pulling on my little black clogs and hanging my stethoscope around my neck as I headed to work each day to care for the dying. It was good work, though grueling. I'd paid off my student debt and was diligently saving for retirement and buying furniture for my tiny urban apartment. Was this success?

Admittedly, my social life at the time was fairly bleak. I had a few friends in town but having come from the Midwest, San Diego wasn't exactly my scene. Weekends consisted of smoking spliffs on the beach and dressing up in hipster threads to listen to surf rock and drink PBRs at the local dive bars. Spirituality was the usual Wednesday night Ashtanga yoga class with some Hindu chanting. I'd been agnostic since leaving the Catholic Church in my teens and I believed there must be *something* out there, some kind of loving intelligence holding this whole thing together, but it was a hazy notion at best.

To others, I seemed happy and had a great life, but I was depressed. Despite the constantly sunny weather, something in me was dying. I'd been in therapy for about six months, trying multiple antidepressants for my quarter-life crisis; something was very wrong with my life, but I had no idea what.

When my family planned Christmas in Costa Rica, I decided to quit my job and backpack alone in Central America to get away and search for answers. I'd been crying out to the universe for change, and something, somewhere heard me. On New Year's Day 2009, I joined a crew of spiritual nomads for a "Raw Medicinal Plants of the Jungle" retreat.

The first three days we bushwhacked through the sweaty, buggy jungle with machetes. We bathed naked in the cool river as a blue morpho butterfly gently floated overhead. We arrived at a cave within a mountaintop nature reserve for our first of many 'cacao ceremonies,' consisting of drinking a strong, bitter mug of psychoactive hot chocolate and connecting with our feelings.

To my surprise, as I breathed into the center of my chest, a lifetime of unfelt emotion and bottled tears cascaded from the depths of my being. I couldn't believe I'd never touched this place of openness, sensitivity, and grief within myself. The others held my hands and beamed unconditional love my way, encouraging my tears. One woman hugged me for an uncomfortably long stretch. "Welcome home, sister." Tears of joy rolled down my cheeks.

What I'd been missing was revealing itself: I'd desperately needed this kind of community. I craved this level of vulnerability and presence, as well as a reverent connection to the natural world. I craved this radical, sing-it-from-the-rooftops aliveness.

For three nights, we did ritualized trance dancing around a great bonfire, dancing with our heartbreak, our fears, and our joy. My body's intelligence was awakening, gaining momentum. Then, our group leader stated that a well-known shaman from Peru was coming for a series of Ayahuasca ceremonies and asked if I wanted to attend.

"What's Ayahuasca?" I inquired, as the name rolled curiously around in my mind, both familiar and foreign. He paused, then asked if I had any experience with magic mushrooms. "Umm, I tried them a few times in college," I replied. With a deep breath and a smile, he told me I would do fine.

Luckily, I knew very little about this mysterious entheogenic brew when I first brought the cup to my lips. I only knew it was immensely powerful and worthy of deep reverence.

Clearly things were happening for other people: deep breaths and sighs fell out of their mouths, their fire-lit bodies rocked side to side. The shaman shook her rattle and sang one "icaro" after the next, the lyrics and melodies a sacred technology to activate the medicine's potential within us.

I went up for my second full cup of the thick, dark medicine and drank it down. Almost instantly, the medicine began to open to me and drew me into her outrageous universe of color, energy, beauty, and terror. The everyday world faded away as I was absorbed into the multidimensional, Technicolor landscape, which felt both threatening in its strangeness, as well as immensely generous and intimate.

Mother Ayahuasca—or Grandmother, as she is called— *knew* me.

I breathed heavier, relaxing into the waves of energy vibrating through every cell of my body as my psyche was awash in the scintillating mystery of beingness. I summoned my strength to keep saying "yes" to the experience, trusting it implicitly. Resisting would surely have been a disaster.

A rippling, undulating energy began to gently course through my body, pulsing and flowing, inspiring me to sway my torso and roll my neck. I found myself sitting on my knees in front of the fire, my back beginning to arch as my pelvis rocked forward and back. My breath deepened and became audible as I swooned, my head thrown back. Each in-breath dug deeper into a reservoir of untouched possibility—pulling at it, rising from it, activating my whole being from the ground up. It was pure, unadulterated eros burning through blockages and resistance.

A growing heat emanated through my body, building in intensity as I undulated with breath and sound. I became a dragon, my torso snakelike. The wings of my arms stretched out, fanning the space around me. My tongue hung out of my mouth while my eyes rolled up in my head. I discovered an inner power and ferocity that almost scared me with its unbounded pleasure. Simultaneously, another part of my awareness was completely at rest, witnessing this unprecedented unfolding with both amusement and fascination. I can easily say *nothing* this energetically, erotically, and viscerally transformative had ever remotely occurred for me.

Embarking on my second ceremony, I had a much better sense of what might unfold. I trusted Aya and was curious where she might take me next, but I was definitely a bit intimidated.

Once again, the second cup rapidly plunged me into wondrous prismatic terror, and I sensed the same snakelike energy. It felt like bright electricity sparking through me, causing random twitches and spasms. My spine seemed to be unwinding from the inside out and my arms and legs moved spontaneously. I became aware of the chronic level of physical and psychological tension I'd grown accustomed to and surrendered myself to the healing intelligence of this energy to disintegrate the tension. As if gently opening a valve, the more I relaxed my resistance the more this vibrance would streak through, bringing with it increasingly dramatic involuntary movements. This crescendoed to an ecstatic flailing of my limbs, head, and spine in all directions at once. It was both a liberation of lifetimes of pain and contraction and a glimpse of eternal freedom, two sides of the coin. Not only was I unafraid, but it felt immensely satisfying and beneficial.

The concerned attendants came over, wondering if I was okay and alarmed because I was flailing a bit too close to the others. They carried me outside to a wooden deck slick with falling rain. Left alone, I flopped about like a fish on the deck of a boat.

Once the motion subsided, I sighed loudly, and profoundly relaxed into gravity, involuting for a timeless moment into stillness. Then it happened. A stream of pure liquid fire ignited within me, immensely powerful and steady, rising through my core from my pelvis. It was profoundly pleasurable, connecting me with a soul-level eroticism that I felt as a radiant lovemaking with existence itself.

Fire flooded my whole being, turning me inside out until it exploded into my third eye, like an orgasm of cosmic dimensions with all of creation. I felt my mind and awareness saturated in the universe's creative impulse. There was a gnostic understanding of the beauty and passion of God's infinite desire to know itself, of the divine play or "lila" that is this reality. I felt a love beyond words stretching to every corner of this universe, as the fabric holding it all. I was shown everything I needed to know: I was God, it was me, it was everything, and everything was truly well, safe, and even perfect. All the challenges, all the triumphs, our sense of separation and liberation are just an expression of the infinite intelligence and creativity of the Godhead. I knew I wouldn't be able to stay in that state forever. The ecstasy was literally more than I could bear.

Coming down from this experience, nestled within the nurturing arms of this community and the splendor of Mother Nature, I was awash in wonder. I cried sweet tears of gratitude that grace had carried me toward this initiation. I called my mother and with excitement cried, "Mom, I *do* believe in God!"

This experience was one I'd integrate for the next three months with that community, living off-grid in the jungle, and then steadily for the last thirteen years since then. I had *felt* my connection to life, to my spirit, and to the reality of love as the basis of all things. Because I knew at the deepest level I was "one" with others and with the planet, my priorities restructured. All I wanted to do was serve in a meaningful way, alleviating suffering and bringing about more beauty and wholeness. I saw my own healing as a fundamental part of the healing of our world. I began to relinquish my Catholic shame around sexuality and see this vibrant life force as the unfolding of God's love itself and as a vehicle for my personal expression of love, vitality, and joy. I was done helping people die. It was my calling to help people truly *live*—full power, full pleasure, full heart.

Since that magical time in the jungle, my life has become a living work of art. I left San Diego to move to Northern California, where I took every training possible on sacred sexuality and transformational coaching. I found a whole tribe of modern mystics who've had their own awakenings to this worldview of sacred interdependence. Together we dance, play, and cry. I became a conscious sexuality coach, and then after a few years, I trained in somatic psychotherapy and became a psychedelic guide for individual and group ceremonies, introducing others to the magnificent healing potential within their own bodies, hearts, and spirits.

That night on the mountain, I experienced the sublime truth of our sacred interconnectedness with each other, with the moon and the stars, and the whole family of plant and animal beings here on this remarkable planet. I understood that we have *everything* we need to create the most abundant, juicy, glorious future imaginable, and it begins within ourselves. I am beyond blessed every day to be doing this sacred work with the most inspiring leaders, entrepreneurs, and visionaries, and living in alignment with my deepest yearnings for our collective evolution.

Bright blessings to you, dear reader.

| 25 |

CAITLIN NARAMORE

A MERMAID TAKES MANHATTAN

THE CARS WERE LINED UP over two blocks, waiting their turn for gas. A large swath of New York was a black box without power. My friend's tiny Brooklyn apartment was packed with a half-dozen refugees from the storm.

It was my first time in New York City, and I'd arrived via a one-way ticket on the tail of Hurricane Sandy. I had nothing to my name but the clothes in my suitcase, $200 in my bank account, and trust the size of the continent I'd just flown over to get here.

Four months earlier …

After a painful breakup, I knew in my bones it was time to escape my home state of California, but I didn't know where or when. Then, literally moments after coming out of a meditation where I was shown a lush, tropical home on an island, I ran into a friend.

"Caitlin," she gushed. "I found our house!"

And so, on a wing and a prayer I purchased a one-way ticket to Kauai—Hawaii's northernmost island—and took up residence in our new home, The Golden Chalice Palace. It felt natural, easy, and graceful.

A number of years before, I'd lived and worked in a cutting-edge science community on the Big Island of Hawaii. We were working on creating a free energy device as a solution to many global energy problems. During that time, my role had been as head chef/kitchen vixen. I spent my mornings swimming with dolphins and my days preparing exotic foods for the staff and visiting Nobel laureates, always surrounded by titans of the mind (our dinner conversations were fit for Einstein himself), and literally living in paradise. But at night, in my dreams, I traveled to New York—always with a sense of purpose.

In one dream, I was a couture designer. In another, a chef for army troops. In yet another, a stealth Jedi roaming the dark streets on some sort of vigilante mission. The scenarios shifted, but it was always New York. The dreams were lucid and real; I woke up feeling like I had actually been there.

Five years, three moves, two countries, and a profound four-year romantic relationship later, I was back in Hawaii—

this time in our home on Kauai. I basked in the silken, tropical air and swam in the wild seas as I grieved the loss of my relationship. I also grieved my Californian roots, without quite knowing why; it just felt like I was at a turning point, and there was no going back.

Enter Laura, self-proclaimed "alien from the future."

I'd never met anyone like her. She knew herself, knew exactly what she wanted, and was both highly integrated and totally erratic. She carried with her a message and energy for humanity that felt like it originated with a more advanced society: a universal, crystalline wisdom. Her hot-pink suitcase was so filled with cameras and gadgets and balled-up clothes that she had to use galactic nebula-printed duct tape to hold it closed. She was, quite literally, outside the box.

Of course, we made fast friends. In a private mastermind session by the pool, she helped me find a path to integration in my own body. She was the answer to my prayers; I finally understood how to pair the science I'd been so steeped in with my physical body and its expression. Her work was like a key in a lock—a unification of the field within.

One day, as we lay together in the sand on Secrets Beach—a two-mile stretch of golden sands accessible only by a steep hiking trail—we talked about what it would be like to live forever on this island. Yes, it was beautiful and magical, but this place felt far removed from the "real world." Staying here would mean perpetual peace and tranquility—but it would also mean missing out on growth and evolution.

As it turned out, Laura's home base was New York City.

By the end of the day, we had decided that I would go with her when she returned home.

I was going to New York—the place I'd dreamed about so vividly for years! Initially, it was going to be a two-week visit. But my inner guidance told me otherwise.

I was terrified. Elated. Shocked. Delirious.

I called my dad and announced my next big move. He was at my stepbrother's game, and as I shared my plans my stepbrother scored a home run. Through the phone, I heard a wild, cacophonous cheer. It felt like all the worlds were celebrating me in that moment—like an arrow of God was pointing me due east to the city of my dreams.

My small self was knee-knocked with fear. My mermaid nature—the part of me so at home on the islands—was like, "New York? You? What the actual fuck?"

But my higher self and her army of angels just *knew*.

So, I bought my ticket and began packing to leave Kauai. Only then did news of the "Frankenstorm of the century" blow in. I began to doubt my decision. Maybe I should just stay here where it was warm, known, and safe! Then, as I was sitting in a seaside sushi restaurant that afternoon with my sister and some friends, a tsunami alarm sounded over the entire island and we were forced to evacuate to higher ground.

Oddly, this strengthened my resolve. My calling to New York was so much bigger than any storm. My life could never be dictated by fear again.

Now, buying a one-way ticket to Kauai, where food abundantly grows on trees and you can pretty much live in a pair of flip-flops and a bikini, is a *very* different beast than buying a one-way ticket to New York City on the eve of winter and on the tail of one of the biggest hurricanes of the century. Two dear island sisters gifted me warm socks on my way out of town, since I didn't actually own any. And then, off I flew—over the Pacific Ocean, over California, over the whole of the United States, and landed at JFK Airport just before dawn.

Half of Manhattan was completely blacked out. The rest was shining like a million diamonds. It was the single most powerful moment of my life.

I started bleeding the moment we landed. "Honey, you're home!" my body announced.

I got a cab and made my way across Brooklyn toward Laura's place.

It was cold. It was dystopian. It was dark. Cars waited in lines two blocks deep for gas. This urban Armageddon stood in total opposition to the idyllic, impossible beauty of the island life I'd just departed. It was so eerie, yet like it was my own somehow.

Trust. Trust. Trust.

I arrived at Laura's apartment to a well-made breakfast and a gaggle of refugees from the storm. And so began seven years in New York.

As power was restored, the crowd departed. However, attempting to live with Laura and her husband in 300 square feet of remodeled brownstone was a disaster. Laura gave me three days to move out.

That $200 in my account was now more like $90. The rooms for rent on Craigslist looked like scenes from a Tim Burton film. I had no idea which neighborhoods to look in. My only friend in this city of eleven million people could no longer house me. My California and Hawaii references didn't apply here. In a moment of despair, I laid down on my tiny bed in Laura's office and wept. It was freezing outside. Homelessness, even for a day or two, was not an option. Nor was going back to California. I had never felt so scared, vulnerable, or lost.

Yet, whatever supernatural force had given me the courage to buy that ticket was still with me. Suddenly, I felt a presence—and then, a hand on my heart.

I have always had a connection to the "other side"—to visions, spirit guides, and wisdom from other realms. But even with so many prior spiritual experiences, I wasn't prepared for what came next.

I was shown a vision of an African Maasai chief. He was tall, glorious, and dressed head to toe in ceremonial garb. His words to me, gentle yet firm, were, "There is a place for you."

In a daze of awe, and with renewed resolve, I returned to the computer to search one more time.

Within minutes, there it was, my room—a sublet on the opposite side of Prospect Park. I knew by the feathers in the photos and the sacred wording used by the tenant that this was "the place for me."

The next morning, when I went to see the apartment, I

was awestruck. The woman who opened the door appeared to be a direct descendant of the tribal leader I had met in my vision. She was of the same stature and poise, and even wore the same wide, circular orange earrings.

I swear it's true. You can't make this stuff up.

Just after finding this sublet, I was also led to a raw food cheffing gig in a forty-second-story apartment overlooking Central Park. However, I hadn't yet started the job and essentially had no money. However, my beautiful new householders knew I was the right fit for the room and agreed to let me pay the two months' rent after I'd been paid for a few dinners.

It was living at a knife's edge. Most people, I know, wouldn't do it. I hardly enjoyed it myself; in fact, it was truly scary at times. But I trusted and kept trusting. As long as I followed my intuitive guidance, I was provided for. One step at a time, I followed that guidance to new living situations, job opportunities, and friendships—until, within a few years, I was making six figures as a private chef and healer for billionaires and celebrities, and I was able to get my own beautiful two-bedroom apartment in the most prestigious neighborhood in Brooklyn.

Laura and I stayed in close contact, and she continued to teach me Universal Health Principles and techniques to "get in my body" like never before. I became part of an incredible group of superhumans. At times I felt I was made of light, so incredible were the breakthroughs we created.

All those dreams years before on the Big Island ... they were all coming true. Of course, I was a chef rather than a shoe designer, but the feeling was the same. I would even find myself on streets and in buildings I had dreamt about all those years back. It was confirmation of my soul's *knowing,* and that trust—even when "evidence" was not evident at all—would always lead me in the right direction.

Seven years into my New York journey, I started to feel another tectonic shift within me. The group of lightworkers I had been part of started disbanding. My private cheffing gigs started to feel tired. And, as much as I loved both the real-world grit and glamor of city life, the ceaseless sirens, relentless concrete, and bracingly cold winters started to wear on me.

Change was coming. I could feel it in my bones.

What's more, I was ready to find my mate and the deep soul love I knew I had been born for. I had been an independent single woman for seven amazing years; now, I was ready to find love again.

What followed was a nine-month stint further up the Hudson River in Beacon, New York. There, I spent more time alone than I had in years, exploring waterfalls, mountains, forests, lakes, orchards, and the grand river itself. I prayed and prayed and prayed, literally sending out a beacon of light from my winter confines in Beacon to guide the perfect partner into my life. I swore to myself and God each time I walked into that apartment that this would be the last time I lived alone.

Enter Alok. I'd had visions of him a decade earlier in meditation. He was on the sales team for a coaching program

I joined in 2018. The forming of our partnership is worthy of an entire chapter in and of itself—but let's just say that there were many romantic moments and a few epic getaways before, suddenly, we were making plans to catapult me and my cat across the country to live with him in the desert hamlet of Tucson, Arizona.

Since then, we've started writing a new chapter that includes many global adventures, the forming of my women's coaching business, Modern Queen, and the opportunity to be a loving godmother/stepmother to Alok's son, Sequoia. We now live in the home of our dreams with two cats, sweeping desert views, and a love I could never have imagined before this experience. We are a testament to what comes when we surrender to a deep trust in destiny.

Follow your soul. Follow your heart. Trust your intuition and go where you're led, against all odds, certainly against all fears that would otherwise hold you back. When you do, worlds within worlds will open for you, and your life will become a living dream.

| 26 |

DIANE VAN BUREN

A REFUGEE FROM MY HEART

MY BRAIN SAID, "I've done *everything right.*"

My husband Robert and I had first met early one morning near my second-year architecture design studio. His red hair flowed to his shoulders. Spirit whispered to me: "With *him*, you'll find out *who you are.*" This love held space for freedom to grow and become.

But after thirty-three years of marriage, I felt miserable and lost. I was facing an empty nest after raising two sons with my husband and winning multiple awards in architecture, landscape design, and art. Nevertheless, I rejected that I'd come all this way for ... *this*?

Behind the clamor of accolades, in quiet moments, I lay awake wondering, "Who *am I*?"

Countless nights I wept quietly, and one night, through hot tears, I whispered to my husband, "I should've lived alone after graduating."

I didn't see the damaging effects of my unhappiness on my marriage until the night I stood shaking, heaving great sobs as I stared at the front door, dumbfounded. Friends called my marriage the "gold standard," and now the man of my dreams had walked out.

But after I finished crying, a sigh came out of me, and I went back to my bed. I felt immediate relief. It was amazing. I was relieved, and it was a surprising relief because for several years my blood had been running ice cold in my veins and I couldn't get warm at night. And just like that, I realized my blood felt comfortingly warm once more.

How had I gotten here?

I grew up exploring indigenous sites and natural wonders in the United States. After age ten, when my parents moved us from Midland, Texas, to Tripoli, Libya, my travel adventures expanded exponentially.

My "normal" was marveling at sea urchins clinging to bubbling reefs, hearing camels grunting outside palm-lined souks, romping amid ancient ruins, spotting leopards lounging in trees, waking to monkeys' calls echoing from treetops, and whispering as waves of elephants slaked their thirst by a moonlit waterhole.

The 1969 coup in Libya led to the U.S. Air Force base and

high school closures. Gaddafi's edict held the surprising gift of attending high school for three years in Rome, Italy. Before my senior year, my folks moved to Sumatra, Indonesia. I traveled with them before returning to Rome.

I was happy in Rome living *La Dolce Vita*. Whatever the goal, I simply took steps, and gradually it would be accomplished. Like architecture school.

After meeting Robert, we eventually moved to New York City, and then to Dallas, Texas, where I happily settled into my role as mother to two sons who'd been born two and a half years apart.

As time passed, I struggled to integrate expat life experiences with architecture. I sought spontaneity in design *and* hand-crafted beauty, but neither "fit." I chased shiny objects, desperately seeking fulfillment and expression—would nothing fit?

My deferred dreams became painful—so I stuffed them down. Those unmet dreams settled in as excruciating sciatica and a herniated disc.

Two back surgeries later, I still couldn't see the way forward. My body and mind were wracked with conflicting ideals: freedom to travel the world and the desire to be a stay-at-home mom and supportive wife.

In 2008, the first spark showed up after the economy tanked. My boys were mostly grown, and I was out of work, feeling ungrounded, miserable, and lost.

A friend called. "Would you be my guide to Italy?"

"Yes!" I answered in a heartbeat.

On this long-awaited return to Rome, tears came to my eyes. Oh, the beauty! The reverence! The love! The mess and the magic all in one! Had I tossed this love aside? How had decades flown by?

Life's meandering currents had swept me far from my soul-nourishing world adventures.

I went on an odyssey to find the answers back to myself.

Going deep within, I asked myself, "How did I get interested in architecture?"

"Ah, cities."

"What makes people fall in love with cities?"

"That's easy: the wonderful *piazzas*, the urban squares! They're magic!"

No professional degree program was available to study urban squares, so I found a Master of Liberal Studies program and enrolled in 2012. The timing helped me survive sorting out what had been eating me from the inside.

Travels feed architecture. I developed an appreciation for the synergies between space, place, and spirit from my wealth of deep travel experiences. What I knew before I'd graduated from college came roaring back into my awareness: I felt cramped. I'd *settled*.

I was raised to minimize risk and focus on results. It wasn't clear how investing in a Master's degree would benefit me, but my husband had encouraged it.

I was looking everywhere outside myself for the solution. But hiding festering unhappiness isn't sustainable.

That is how I'd ended up here.

I was shocked that I'd manifested a separation, and when I'd hugged my husband before he walked away, I felt my heart pancake as it flattened from squeezing so hard. There was enormous feeling in our parting. My heart raced: it was "Broken Heart Syndrome."

I struggled to string together three hours of sleep. Anguish left me howling out the last bit of energy before sleeping. In my waking hours, my mind raced 24/7 to find the solution to my problem.

"We can prescribe antidepressants for you," my cardiologist offered.

"No, thank you." I looked him in the eye. "I think I have a good reason to be depressed. I want to be present to the process of healing."

Through it all, I continued my Master's studies. One of my professors with health challenges requested rides home after class and I volunteered several times. On one occasion driving him home, I shared aspirations and my unclear direction beyond graduation. His words were worth more than my entire graduate investment: "You must live *expansively*."

The semester end allowed me to rejoin my Italian Conversation Meetup in a restaurant. I arrived to find conversations in full swing. Then a new couple arrived and, with no space at the table, we took a booth nearby.

At length, they revealed they were recruiters from the University of Texas. They invited me to teach Italian, and I was giddy with joy.

Subsequently, they invited me to meet the Advanced

Italian instructor. This well-groomed gentleman, about my father's age, began sharing his history as a geologist in various countries in Africa, including that he'd lived in Tripoli, Libya. My eyes widened.

He continued, "But how did you come to speak Italian?"

"I lived in Tripoli, too!"

"Did you go to OCS [Oil Companies School]?"

"Yes."

He shared that his daughter went there. She was my Italian friend from Tripoli.

"Where does she live now?" I asked.

She lived nearby!

In a matter of weeks, we met, and it was a joyous reunion. Due to not having moving addresses, I'd lost all my treasured expat friendships, and it weighed heavily on me. With our reunion, I felt relief and a healing surge of intentional reintegration. I experienced a massive reality shift and a new lightness in my being. I was learning to follow my intuition and look within myself.

Next, I followed my intuition to study abroad for an Art History course in Italy. *"Perche no?/*Why not?" I delighted in Italy's beauty and felt at home in Rome.

One day, as I admired the architecture surrounding one piazza, a motorcyclist entered from the left, disappeared behind the building opposite the church, and reappeared on the right.

Eureka! The Piazza is Theater! My capstone paper all but wrote itself.

My capstone shared the beauty and wonder of these highly evolved, magical places. I celebrated with my (separated) husband, my Italian friend, and her husband. More was healing: I strengthened my sense of accomplishment, appreciation, and fulfillment.

After graduation, I vowed to visit Italy at least once every year. My friend Peter (who taught sculpture at my high school) asked, "Would you like to have an art exhibit in Rome?" The answer was clear.

Before leaving for Rome, I applied for a ceramics residency there. On the day I arrived, I received an email that I'd been accepted! Rome would be my home for six weeks, back in my old neighborhood, Trastevere, from my high school days.

One rainy evening after a long day working with clay, I decided to try a new place to eat nearby. I walked over to Piazza di San Cosimato and into a warmly lit, bustling trattoria.

As the evening passed, I struck up a new friendship with a young lady who lived on my street. Later, she invited me to a Pilates class. "We'll have to meet someplace because it's really hard to find," she told me.

Once she gave me the address, I was elated! "I know *exactly* where it is! It's by my ceramics studio!"

It was the very place I'd wondered about, as I passed it several times a week. I was growing my community and creating my own life.

This began my addiction to the ballet-like Pilates at a studio deep in Rome's labyrinth.

Before returning home, I shared a book I'd written with Harvard mentor and Forum School Professor Edward Steinberg. We spoke about how life unfolds for us. With his twinkling eyes and soft voice, he shared, "People say, 'I'll believe it when I see it.' Yet, very often it happens this way: when you believe it, you see it."

It took some time before I realized my book was also the foundation of my coaching program: to evolve expansively and thrive in fulfilling lives—all our days!

Many women leaders have endured inner turmoil as bearers of deferred dreams … indefinitely.

"Would I live the remainder of my life alone?" I wondered. I enjoyed solitude, but I also loved my husband. At family gatherings, we hugged and said, "I love you." We got each other: he devoted himself to public buildings; I devoted myself to public spaces. I had gained freedom in clarity. I suggested to Robert that we meet, as we occasionally did for lunch. Our conversation was amicable.

I shifted. "If there's nothing left for us moving forward, we may as well divvy the finances and get the paperwork done," I said. His eyes welled up. He'd been patiently waiting for years. I was stunned and we both agreed to get with a counselor to sort things out. I knew exactly who to call and she has helped us elevate our communication to an entirely new level of healthy affection and self-love. I am grateful to be reunited with Robert and to continue our journey of healing, growth, and joy.

Everything came together and it all became possible by aligning with my voice, my authenticity, and my full self-expression—because nothing less than full self-expression will do. A mind that has expanded cannot shrink.

Manifesting and creating my ideal future comes through following intuition, dreaming forward, taking baby steps, and allowing it to unfold in divine timing

I had to break through my subconscious beliefs that safety came in hiding and fitting in. I took a huge risk to break with my old way of being, to recognize the patterns, and to integrate practices that allowed me to rise above my perceived limits.

Ironically, being a misfit is my superpower. What makes me limitless are my world experiences to facilitate experiencing the beauty and ancient wisdom in other cultures around the world.

The highest benefit of travel comes in exploring places that elevate peoples' experiences, spark imagination, connect them to higher-level thinking, and reveal ingenuity. This is what I experienced: the urban square, the piazza, has the potential to align us with our unique genius. The basis of Self-Leadership is my expert niche: coaching transformational leadership through The Transformational Power of Place!

What uplifts my vision and mission in the world is propelling inventive leadership as we "age." Experiencing the beauty and vibrance in the world's most beloved places builds harmony and humanity as we appreciate our diversity. World travel is the best education. Travel refines the senses and cultivates understanding. Beauty elevates consciousness.

Each of us can access our authenticity, live expansively,

and live agelessly as bold sages, owning our wisdom and experience, and contributing with deep meaning—all our lives.

| 27 |

ESTHER ALLEY
MYSTICAL
MIRACLES

EGYPT: THE GATEWAY to my soul.

I remember when my feet first touched the ground there in 1996. I was traveling with a group that was following a Māori elder from New Zealand. When we landed in Cairo, I could feel the energy; the ground was pulsing, and the energy of that great land was absorbed into my body. I experienced the power of the ancient beings who once walked there, and whose essences are still accessible in the higher densities. I felt as if I was walking between worlds.

That trip helped awaken me to the truth that I am a multi-dimensional being having a human experience. Just as I seemed to recognize and resonate with the land, the people in both lower and upper Egypt seemed to recognize my energy. They were giving me gifts of all kinds—a scarf, beaded necklaces, statues, and more—and while I couldn't explain what they were seeing in me, I knew I was home.

Since then, I've been called back to Egypt many times; each visit has been a deep and profound experience. For the last ten years, I've journeyed there at least once a year, usually with a group of light beings, to do soul-making work.

This past year, as I was mentally preparing for my annual trip, my higher self said to me, "Go to Rythmia first."

That inner voice has been my savior more times than I can remember—so, of course, I listened.

For those unfamiliar, Rythmia is an upscale resort in Guanacaste, Costa Rica, designed for people who want to experience inner spiritual journeys, soul healing, and freedom from addiction (of any kind) through Ayahuasca ceremonies. I had heard about Rythmia from a girlfriend who came on my Egypt trip in 2019. I had experienced Ayahuasca with an Ecuadorian shaman in 2017, so I was familiar with what was possible through plant medicine. So, when I got the calling to do the medicine again, I knew there was something that Spirit wanted me to know or experience before I made this particular trip to Egypt.

I sensed that this was going to be a very personal and special trip for me; I had gotten messages from different spiritual guides as well as friends about the experiences I would have on this trip. One of my spiritual friends dreamed of me in a temple doing spiritual work, but she didn't know where in Egypt the temple was.

My Egypt trip would be happening in November, so I booked my journey to Rythmia in late May. Almost immediately, Spirit told me to switch to a vegan diet and start purifying my energy.

When I got to Costa Rica, the experience was eye-opening. My revelations while in the medicine were major. I experienced a healing of my heart by way of an energetic open-heart surgery by a group of Divine Beings. They told me to take my daughter and grandsons out of my heart and give them to Spirit, because my worry and concern for them was killing my heart. I was also shown people in my life that I needed to bring back to Rythmia for their own healing.

The most significant reveal, however, was about my home. I was in a fourteen-year legal battle over a bad loan on the house I'd bought almost thirty years ago, and it had been consuming a lot of my energy. I was told to release the house and everything that tied me to it because Spirit had something greater for me.

I was being separated from every earthly thing with which I identified. It felt really scary, but it was freeing at the same time. Without that house tying me down, I felt like I could do *anything*. I remember this distinct feeling that I didn't even need to go back to my house because it didn't even feel like mine anymore. I couldn't think of anything inside the house important enough for me to go back for. I was free; I was limitless. Anything I required would be provided for me.

During that week at Rythmia, I let go of burdens I didn't even know I was carrying. When I got off the plane in the city where I'd been living for more than three decades, I no longer felt attached to the place. There was nothing left there for me, and it was only a matter of time before I would move on. I had no clue where I was supposed to go, or when; I just knew I would be moving.

It was a true test of my faith. Like so many times before, I was stepping into the void and trusting the universe to hold me up.

The idea of "Living by faith" began to grow within me after my first near-death experience at the age of twenty-three. It was then that I stepped on the spiritual path. These days, I consult with and trust the Universe in every situation in my life. I've learned to completely surrender the moment a challenge or opportunity arises and go deep within my being to find the courage to keep going. This latest experience was no different.

After my first trip to Rythmia, I was guided to bring groups of people back to Costa Rica to experience the healing of plant medicine. I traveled to Costa Rica a total of five times that year! On one of those trips, I met a guy named Alok. We talked only briefly and didn't even exchange information. I knew the encounter was meaningful, but I didn't give it too much thought because I was still preoccupied with the messages I'd received on my first Costa Rica trip regarding my living situation. Even after all the trips and doing more plant medicine, I still had no clue about what I was supposed to be doing, what was next for me, or when or where I was supposed to be moving.

My trip to Egypt that fall was all I anticipated it to be and more. Each time I go to Egypt I have intense spiritual revelations and visions, but this trip was even more so. One of the most mystical experiences happened in a special temple that was off-limits to the public. In fact, this temple wasn't even on our itinerary; our guide decided spontaneously to take us there. It turned out to be the temple that my spiritual friend had seen in her vision. Even though I had never been there in this lifetime, I magically knew my way around inside. Everything about it was so familiar to me. There were even rooms I couldn't go into because the energy in them was so strong.

This was the temple of Khonshu, God of the Moon. This was a key connection for me personally, and many questions were answered here. I had been in search of where the Avenue of the Sphinx started. I had a memory of walking from Karnak to Luxor on the Avenue of the Sphinx. The memory was so strong that I thought it had happened on my first trip to Egypt, but because there were modern roads that crisscrossed the avenue and broke it up, I could see that was impossible. I couldn't find the start of the Avenue, and for years no one I asked knew where it began.

Well, the Avenue began at this temple. At that point, it all became clear: I was remembering a past life. I came home feeling like many parts of myself had been reclaimed.

Yet, despite all the answers I got in Egypt, I still had no

idea where and when I was moving, or what I was supposed to do next.

More magic began to unfold when I arrived back in the United States, but it was very subtle. I felt the Universe starting to move the puzzle pieces of my life. The winds of change were swirling around me, but I knew I had to stay focused and faithful. I was aware of the move I would need to make, but I felt like I was in limbo. My business wasn't growing as fast as I desired, and the future seemed foggy and unclear. Some days I awoke in a full-on sweaty panic and had to dig deep into my spiritual toolbox to find my equilibrium.

My sister Ruth had passed away while I was traveling; she was my anchor, and being alone without a physical person to lean on was extremely difficult for me. I would have days of complete withdrawal from the world, so I turned to my coaching to help me move forward. I was at a time in my life when, according to society, I should have been enjoying retirement, traveling for leisure, and enjoying my grandkids. None of that was happening in my life. I felt so driven; I knew I had so much more to give. I felt that my spiritual coaching business was the way I would find my purpose. I felt the light within me ignite when I worked with my clients. The passion that had somehow eluded me in past careers was finally growing in me.

I had started following Alok Appadurai (the guy I'd met at Rythmia) on social media. He piqued my interest as to what was possible for me and my business, and Egypt had confirmed that I was ready for more. When he asked me to join his four-month intensive program, I was very excited, but still without any of the answers I was seeking from the Universe.

In Alok's program, I began learning so much about my business, myself, and how to create more movement in my life. For the first time, I began to fully embrace my powers and spiritual gifts, appreciate the work I was doing, and understand how I was contributing to others and the planet day by day, moment by moment. I began to feel the shift. Magically, several new clients came on board, and I had a record-setting month in my business.

As all of this unfolded, I began to sense my own courage in moving to the forefront of my being. This was something new; I had stepped into my power. This process of being elevated to another level in my life seemed to just be happening, in a matter-of-fact way, but I knew the energy was fueling the changes. Over and over, I surrendered to the process. I had to—it was too esoteric to do otherwise.

One pivotal moment came during one of Alok's group meetings. He told me what he thought was the minimum price I should be charging for my coaching services. When he said that number, I couldn't even imagine it, let alone ask anyone to pay me that. As a Black woman, I had never been exposed to this kind of thinking, nor had I ever dared to dream that big. Even though I knew that the Universe is unlimited and that it is always conspiring for my highest and greatest good, this was another level.

When I got off that call, my head was reeling. Suddenly, a

client I had worked with for years came to mind. This client would get big annual bonuses, and every year she would give me a bonus, too. When I added up all those bonuses, I realized *I had already been paid the amount Alok had suggested I should charge.* It was like a miracle happened in that moment. I could see myself changed right then and there as I accepted that I was, in fact, worth that much and more. This went beyond any intellectual understanding. In that moment, I was limitless—just like the Universe. I saw my true worth for the first time ever in my life. The "something greater" I'd been calling in was unfolding right before my eyes.

Within a week, I landed a client at my new rate. I could clearly see how I had been limiting myself by not recognizing and not valuing the wisdom and experience I brought to the table and the awesome work I was doing in the world. Once I found the courage to act on my new understanding of who I am *being*, it was easy for me to help my clients and others see this in themselves.

Then, another piece of the puzzle fell into place. That December, the real estate company who was handling the negotiations for my house called and offered me cash for keys.

That house had served me well. For fourteen years, I'd battled with the courts to keep it. It wasn't until the Universe said, *Let it go*, I have something greater for you, that I was willing to cede that fight. Now, not only was I letting it go but I was also getting paid to do so.

After releasing the house, I moved across the country to a house in the city of Mount Rainier, Maryland. I'd never heard of this city, but Mount Rainier was the name of the peak I had seen every morning for the last thirty years from the kitchen window of my previous home. That was another confirmation of the something greater.

I have found and am living my purpose. My business is growing in a direction that allows me to help others step into their greatness and live their best lives. My "something greater" is to help as many light workers and light warriors as possible to awaken. My own magical, mystical journey now helps me inspire others to let their lights shine.

ABOUT ALOK APPADURAI

ALOK APPADURAI is the Founder and CEO of Uplift Millions and the *Wall Street Journal* bestselling author of *Maximum Impact Potential: How to Own Your Value, Become a Wealth Circulator, and Uplift Millions.*

Alok was born in Philadelphia, PA in 1978 and has dedicated his life to making a positive impact in the world. He's launched four impact-driven companies, three in the industries of clean energy, global media for women, and sustainable clothing, as well as his most recent company, Uplift Millions, a coaching company for entrepreneurs who value people, planet, and profit.

He graduated from Wesleyan University in 2000, where

he built his own major combining Economics, History & Literature, and then went on to teach third through sixth grades in New York City before launching his career in social entrepreneurship.

In 2015, Alok gave a TEDx Talk on feeding hundreds of thousands of emergency meals to people in need. He was nominated for the Gifted Citizen award, has been recognized by the Ashoka Foundation's "Threads For Thought" competition, and has been a speaker for multiple social entrepreneurship summits and events.

Much of Alok's professional career has been spent creating businesses that uplift women, in particular. He believes the world gets better when more money flows through more women.

Alok's travels to more than thirty countries on five continents (including visits to the Mother Teresa House in Calcutta and the slums of Johannesburg), combined with growing up in West Philadelphia, have shaped his dedication to making other people's lives better, but the most transformative day of his life thus far was the day his son, Sequoia, was born.

Alok wears his heart on his sleeve, enjoys making hand-poured candles, and loves to ski. His favorite food is masala dosa, and whenever he eats Ben & Jerry's ice cream, he thinks of his late mother, Carol.

Learn more about Alok at upliftmillions.com.

ABOUT THE AUTHORS

KARISSA ADKINS is a former marketing and HR professional turned two-time entrepreneur, Certified Badass Coach, and champion for women's mental and physical health. Karissa is the voice behind the award-winning BossUp Babes Podcast, TV personality, award-winning international speaker, and 2X international bestselling author. Karissa has been featured on networks such as ABC, CBC, USA Today, and NBC for her expertise in empowering and motivating women to get fit and stay healthy. She has been featured on the covers of *2Inspire Health* and *Your Success* magazine. Referred to as America's BossUp Babe and the Queen of Habit Change, Karissa is known for her fierce personality, insane levels of passion, high-level strategies, and a no-BS approach to living healthy, happy, and wealthy, as she transforms women's mindsets, bodies, and lifestyles. Learn more at 365dailyhustle.com

ESTHER ALLEY is an Intuitive Spiritual Life Coach, author, and speaker. After thirty years in the public and corporate sector, Esther returned to school to become a certified Life Coach at InviteChange Coaching School and is certified by the International Coaching Federation (ICF). Esther also had three years of training at InnerVision Institute for Spiritual Development. As a result of her intuitive spiritual life coaching program, her clients experience lasting transformation that opens up new possibilities in their lives. They shift from confusion to clarity; from restraint to freedom; from fear to courage; and from doubt to a deep knowing. She has been coaching and helping people since 2007. Here website: www.estherjones-alley.com

JANA ALONSO is an English and Spanish speaker, integrative healing expert, bestselling author, and the founder of The School of Integrative Healing. Integrative Healing (IH) is a unified, all-encompassing system of multi-modality and dimensional healing, ten years in the making, that offers a long-term approach to true, holistic transformation. IH was born from the concept of synergy, and that unity makes us stronger than separation. The combination of many healing modalities (from physical hormonal healing all the way to energetic shamanic healing) makes this system of healing so unique, effective, and life-changing. Jana lives and works in the forest in Ibiza, with her partner, pitbull, and bossy Siamese cat. Find out more at theschoolofintegrativehealing.com.

ADAM BARAZ is a Somatic Life-Coach, bodyworker, and meditation teacher, who teaches people how to heal their trauma and "transform their life from the inside out." He received his degree in Somatic Psychology from Naropa University, is a licensed professional bodyworker with multi-year training in Counseling Psychology, Somatic Experiencing (SE), and Cranial-Sacral Therapy. Son of meditation teacher, James Baraz, Adam discovered meditation at age seven, and has spent over a decade studying Buddhist philosophy under meditation masters in the Tibetan tradition. Adam has dedicated over a year of his life to intensive meditation retreats, including sixty-three days alone in total darkness. Adam enjoys surfing big waves in Maui, and playing chess with friends. Learn more at samadhibodywork.com

TONI BERGINS is on a mission to get people into their bodies, to feel, heal, expand their bandwidth, end perfectionism, stop the "not good enough" crisis, and inspire people to express their authentic uniqueness in a world that needs all our healing now. Toni, MEd, founder and director of JourneyDance®, is an artistic alchemist and passionate catalyst for people to transform their angst into art and their vulnerability into strength. Over the past twenty-five years, she has helped thousands of people find a new sense of self-esteem, inner wisdom, emotional health, spiritual practice, and total well-being. She leads an international team of over

1,000 JourneyDance Leaders, has a popular instructional JourneyDance DVD, a series of online courses, and a private practice in her Embodied Transformations Method. She is a recording artist and one-person show creator with her stories and original music. Her sense of humor and authenticity makes JourneyDance® programs accessible to all. Visit journeydance.com to learn more.

DANIELLA COTREAU has transformed the lives of thousands of entrepreneurs to become visionary leaders who create businesses they love and that impact the world. She is a heart-based leadership coach, spiritual mentor, consultant, embodiment expert and business mentor with twenty-plus years of experience. She is the founder Heart Wisdom Leadership Academy® and creator of Body Temple Yoga® Method. Daniella teaches leaders heart-led techniques to embody in their life and leadership for the greatest success and fulfillment. She leads group programs and private mastermind retreats in personal transformation and heart-based business evolution in locations across the globe. Learn more at daniellac.com

DEREK COZZENS is a transformational leader who is focused on bringing people together to solve some of the most pressing challenges facing the world today. He specializes in helping powerful individuals, teams, companies, and world leaders to transform the way we do business to restore, regenerate, and sustain the water, air, and soil on the planet and bring diversity and inclusion into private equity. Derek is a successful business and team leader who has been CEO, CFO, and COO of numerous private equity portfolio companies as well as an investor in dozens of real estate ventures personally. He helps companies maximize efficiency, profit, and cashflow while implementing best-in-class practices to scale and take organizations to the next level and beyond. Find him on LinkedIn @derek-cozzens-65273820.

DANIEL DIAZ is a performance and mindset specialist. His many layers of transformation are told throughout stories of his life. From drug dealing to America's top-rated food truck by *Forbes* magazine. From stressed out, burnt out, overwhelmed entrepreneur, to personal development master now listed as top ten performance coach by Yahoo Finance. From being immobilized through grueling back injuries to becoming an ultra-athlete. Danny is the living example that anything is possible. His mission is to help others discover, and live into, their limitless potential and possibilities in life. Learn more at iamdanieldiaz.com.

DOMINEY DREW is a spiritual advisor, author, speaker, and intuitive healer. High performers in every industry hire her to break down the current paradigms in their inner world which keep them from real fulfillment and maximum impact. Dominey is the premier in rapid results coaching; her direct, intuitive approach is unlike anything else in the industry. Through a process of profound self-discovery, she solves in mere minutes issues that have carried on for decades. She's been featured in *Forbes* and *Entrepreneur* magazine for her work, and now travels the world teaching those who seek massive transformation. Dominey has dived to the depths of her own soul countless times, through seemingly endless layers of trauma, to rise like a phoenix into a default state of effortless joy. Now, she exists every day in flow and ease, and her passion is teaching others to do the same. Visit domineydrew.com.

KATHLEEN FRIEND, MD is a child psychiatrist on a mission to change the paradigm in her field and put one million children in the Greatness Chair. She is the author of two children's books, *The Greatness Chair* and *Sarah in the Greatness Chair,* and a book for parents and teachers called *The Greatness Chair Solution*, which teaches a simple, accessible method to bring out the best in children. *The Greatness Chair* has been translated into Hebrew and Spanish and will be available in 2023. Dr. Friend is an international speaker, musician, and Heart Rhythm Meditation teacher for IAM Heart, a global meditation school dedicated to fostering the culture of the heart. She is a strong advocate for following the passions in one's heart and seeing the strengths in all. Learn more about her work at greatnesschair.com.

LESLIE GRACE, RN is a highly trained and experienced psychedelic integration guide who works with leaders, entrepreneurs, and visionaries to unlock their highest calling. Building on her foundation as a registered nurse, and her Bachelor's in Biopsychology, Leslie now integrates psychedelic healing, somatic therapy, and sacred sexuality teachings in her practice. Over the past decade, she's worked with thousands of souls through her private and group programs to expand their consciousness, self-love, and joy in life. Leslie currently lives in the San Francisco Bay Area. Explore your potential at lesliegrace.co.

MIKE ISKANDER is wondering: What if you could travel back in time to every age of your life? What would you say to those younger versions of yourself? What would you learn about who you were, who you want to become, and who you truly are today? That whimsical what-if inspired TEDx speaker Mike Iskandar to create Time Travel Journeys—a powerful new approach to personal development and team-building that guides schools, organizations, and companies to explore how the past and future can transform the present epidemic of anxiety, depression, and burnout into deeper joy, compassion, confidence, and connection. Learn more at timetraveljourneys.com.

TOM LADEGAARD, ESQ. is a Southern California business attorney specializing in trademarks and litigation, in his nineteenth year of practice. When Tom isn't working or plotting world domination, he can be found experimenting in the kitchen, hiking the trails around San Diego, tending to his garden, mastering his guitar and vocals, or playing board games with his teenagers. Learn more at ladegaardlaw.com.

SARAH B. LANGE, MSW is among the nonprofit sector's top revenue generators, having raised over $90 million! Using innovative approaches, she has worked with over 200 nonprofits to raise money, build stronger boards, chart an exciting course for the future, and brag about the good work they're doing. Sarah has served as an adjunct professor at Clark University, Boston University, Worcester State University, and the University of Massachusetts, Boston. Her book, *The Field Guide to Nonprofit Fundraising* (Praeger), was published in December 2017. Her BA is from Colgate University; her Masters is from BU School of Social Work. To learn more, please visit sarahblange.com

LAUNA MARTIN, mentor and speaker, brings twenty years of experience in the art of relationship to leaders who desire life that makes meaning, not just business that makes money. If Betty White and Buddha had a baby, Launa is their love child. Her proven methods and superpowers of wit, wisdom, levity, and love guide daring humans to a path of purpose. Often called the "Power Behind the Throne," she's the founder of Morpha Multidimensional Leadership Firm, trusted as the safe space where decision-makers lay down their armor to transform into the ultimate people, partners, and parents. Visit morpha.vip to learn more.

JULIA MIKK is an internationally renowned healer, teacher, and bestselling author, and the founder of the SOLignment Institute with certified facilitators in many countries. Unlike any other healing work, SOLignment Process is very powerful, incredibly efficient, and quick in its ability to break through stagnant patterns. Julia's clients come from all over the world to receive deep emotional healing, and embody courage to live their soul purpose. She masterfully weaves concepts of non-duality, breathwork, shamanic studies, biodynamic craniosacral therapy, and pre- and perinatal psychology to create liberation from old patterns that manifest as lack, worry, fear or chronic health issues in one's life. Learn more at solignment.com.

LIAT NADLER is a nutritionist, dietitian, health and food relationship expert, influencer, and coach. She is the founder of Fabulous Healing Nutrition & Wellness, a retired engineer, a wife, and a mother. Liat founded Fabulous Healing Nutrition & Wellness to help results-driven females get their glow, increase their confidence and energy, and step into their unstoppable, sexy, badass selves! Liat is dedicated to helping committed, busy women end the endless yo-yo dieting cycles, clear their skin from persistent conditions, and heal their gut. The end result? They step into a better, more energetic, and confident version of themselves. Learn more at www.fabuloushealing.com.

CAITLIN NARAMORE is a business coach and consultant for spiritually and holistically based entrepreneurs. She is the founder and CEO of Modern Queen LLC. Caitlin helps her clients achieve greater well-being and success in both their professional and personal lives, bridging heaven and earth through pleasurable and sustainable profit. Previously, Caitlin was a chef for billionaires, scientists, authors, and rockstars, and still adores making magical cakes on the regular. Caitlin is also a healer, poet, singer and artist, and partner of Alok Appadurai. Discover more at caitlinnaramore.com.

JERRY NARANJO is a passionate, engaging, innovative, and heart-centered business leader with over thirty years of experience. He has been a pioneer in the civil construction industry in Colorado, leading his firm to build some of the state's most iconic and innovative river restoration projects. Jerry is a trusted advisor to employees and clients alike, guiding them with insights on business matters, scaling, operations, organizational management, visionary leadership, and relentless execution. His unique roadmap to success is based on positivity, authentic relationships, and replacing goals with actions. Learn more at naranjocg.com

DEBRA RUBIN, MA, CMT, RYT is a Master Coach, Movement Alchemist, and internationally renowned facilitator and performer. She has her MA in Holistic Health from JFK University, BA in Psychology & Pre-Med from Princeton University, and twenty years of study and client care in mind-body medicine, somatics, yoga, fascia and trauma release from both Eastern and Western disciplines. Deb is CEO of Shakti Embodied Feminine Leadership Academy, guiding women to move beyond limits, unlock full body freedom and optimal movement, ignite their feminine power, and create their limitless, prosperous life. The creator of Dance Therapeutics Movement Mastery System, she is published in *Yoga Journal* and lives in Los Angeles. Visit debrubindancetherapeutics.com.

GIGI ABDEL-SAMED, MD, MBA, FACEP is a Board-certified Emergency Medicine Physician who has treated thousands of patients in her almost twenty-eight years in practice. She is a recognized speaker and transformational coach, with an MBA. Dr. Gigi is the creator of Medical School for the Soul, an innovative curriculum for medical students and healthcare practitioners that brings satisfaction throughout their careers, prevents burnout while increasing revenue and patient satisfaction. Her legacy is to return the heart to healthcare, one medical school class at a time, one physician at a time. Learn more at drgigisamed.com.

KARI SCHWEAR is an Executive Lifestyle Coach, speaker, and corporate trainer. She's also a certified GiANT Worldwide guide, specializing in leader transformation and development. Kari coauthored the book, The *Successful Mind: Tools for Living a Purposeful, Productive, and Happy Life,* published in 2020. As a former "gray-area drinker," Kari founded GrayTonic in 2018 after her own experience of "living in the gray" led her to the service of others. Her zone of genius is habit change, communication, leadership development, and intentional living. Kari holds certifications in Motivational Interviewing, Life Coaching, NLP, and several trauma courses through the NICABM. Discover Kari's work at graytonic.com

PAIGE STAPLETON is an internationally renowned author, speaker, mentor, and founder of Paige Stapleton Coaching. She empowers service-based women entrepreneurs to have more success with greater ease and fun—while remaining true to themselves. Paige is passionate about helping others learn to sell with integrity and heart. For over fifteen years, she has guided thousands of heart-centered, mission-driven entrepreneurs to monetize their passion and purpose. During the "Great Recession," she built a six-figure business in eight months and scaled it to multiple six-figures just ten months later! Paige has supported multiple seven-figure business owners and coaches by closing over $8 million in coaching services for them. Paige currently lives in North Carolina with the love of her life, Brian Stark, and their Australian Shepherd, Bodhi. Learn more at paigestapleton.com.

EMILY ESTHER (SUSSELL) is an entrepreneur, coach, and professional copywriter. A yoga teacher and lifelong enthusiast of all contemplative and somatic practices, she centers the values of embodiment and transformation in all her work. Emily holds a Master's degree in Therapeutic Recreation. She was born, raised, and lived for thirty years in New York City and today resides amongst the redwoods in Northern California. Visit emily-esther.com.

DIANE VAN BUREN is a coach, transformational speaker, and author of *Enlightened Rome: Discover the Magic of Piazzas and Public Spaces in Rome, Italy.* Her earliest explorations included visiting indigenous sacred sites and natural spectacles. At age ten, living in Tripoli, Libya, opened a world of travels spanning millennia. She has visited over forty countries and loves languages. Despite awards and successes practicing architecture in New York City and Dallas, Texas, her passion didn't fit in. Conforming cost dearly. Reclaiming joy, she focused on experiencing energy in sacred spaces, and shares world treasures to transform lives. Diane is an author, speaker, and Evolution Mentor™ for successful women leaders. Along deep travels, they thrive on their own terms, all their lives. Learn more at dianevanburen.com.

DR. PETER WISHNIE has practiced podiatry in central New Jersey for over thirty-three years. He completed his undergraduate studies at Stony Brook University in Long Island, New York, then studied podiatric medicine at the California College of Podiatric Medicine (now called The California School of Podiatric Medicine at Samuel Merritt

University). Dr. Wishnie had lectured on many different topics of practice management both nationally and internationally. He recently sold his podiatry practice in order to focus on coaching practice owners to scale their practices in order to create the life they desire. He has three sons, Samuel, Alec, and Benjamin, and an amazing fiancé, Jaimie. He enjoys all sports, especially baseball and football. He's an avid concert goer and enjoys going to the gym. He lives in Somerville, New Jersey. Learn more at stopfootpainfast.com.

KAREN WRIGHT is a master Executive Coach, a thought leader in the global coaching profession, a keynote speaker, and the founder of Parachute Executive Coaching. Author of *The Complete Executive: The 10-Step System for Great Leadership Performance* and *The Accidental Alpha Woman: The Guide to Thriving When Life Feels Overwhelming*, Karen and her team work with leaders who truly want to create workplaces where humans can thrive. Karen is a Canadian who can just as easily be found in Paris or anywhere in the world where there is great art, music, and food. Find out more at parachuteexecutive-coaching.com and accidentalalpha.com

ABOUT THE PUBLISHER

FOUNDED IN 2021 by Bryna Haynes, WorldChangers Media is a boutique publishing company focused on "Ideas for Impact." We know that great books change lives, topple outdated paradigms, and build movements. Our commitment is to deliver superior-quality transformational nonfiction by, and for, the next generation of thought leaders.

Ready to write and publish your thought leadership book with us? Learn more at www.WorldChangers.Media.

CPSIA information can be obtained
at www.ICGtesting.com
Printed in the USA
JSHW021023030523
41182JS00001B/5

9 781955 811446